COOKING *with* *Marianne*

Seasonal Recipes that Bring Health & Joy to Your Table

By
Marianne McCarroll

Published in 2016
Printed by CreateSpace
Available from Amazon.com and other online stores

ISBN-13: 978-1532937415
ISBN-10: 1532937415

NOTES:

- All references in recipes regarding cooking temperature are presented in degrees Farenheit.

- Marianne's Pantry website (www.mariannespantry.com) was the source for the recipes, tips, and most of the photos in this cookbook.

- All photographs were taken wby Marianne McCarroll, except as noted below:

    © Lisa Merrill (www.merrillimages.com)
    Pgs. i, ii, 2, 4, 5, 6, 10, 13, 15, 16, 17, 19, 27, 32, 36 ,37, 38, 39, 40, 42 (cycling and hiking), 43, 45, 48, 60, 63, 66, 68, 70 (melon), 72, 73, 74, 76, 78, 80, 81, 92, 94, 95, 104, 113, 116, 119, 127 (chilis), 129, 135, 136, 137, 138, 142, 143, 155, 156, 157 (mint), 158

    © John Merrill (www.merrillimages.com) Pgs. ii, 20

    © Gregory A. Green (ggreen@owlridgenrc.com) Pgs. 7, 45, 50, 59, 77, 79, 93, 114, 127 (red lentils) 134, 161

    © Stuart Westmorland (www.stuartwestmorland.com): Pg. 1

    © Mond 'Image/DanitaDelimont.com: Pg. 121

    © Brian Jannsen/DanitaDelimont.com: Pg. 159

    © Chuck Haney/DanitaDelimont.com: Pg. 14

    © joannatkaczuk/iStock.com: Pg. 91

    © kabVisio/iStock.com: Pg. 52

    © YinYang/iStock.com: Pg. 64

    © Valvirga/iStock.com: Pg. 110

    © Charles Islander/iStock.com: Pg. 111

    © Valentyn Volkov/iStock.com: Pg. 154

    © Catharine Simon: Pg. 122

    © Paula Doe: Pg. 126

- Editing and proofreading by:

    Susan Carlson, Sarah Daniels, Nancy Davis, Danita Delimont, Elisabeth Jaffe, Jane Vial Jaffe, Bill McCarroll, Lisa Merrill, Marcia Repaci, Heidi Russell, Catharine Simon, Laurian Toland

- Book design by Marcia Repaci, North Creek Design

A Marianne McCarroll Memorial Scholarship will be awarded annually to a student in the Culinary Arts Program at San Joaquin Delta College in Stockton, California, and a donation to the fund is included in the price of this cookbook.

This cookbook is dedicated to Marianne's husband, Dave, and her parents, Bill and Chantal.

❧ Foreward ❧

I often think of Marianne while cooking. We created many delicious meals throughout our long friendship, nourishing our bodies and souls while enjoying skiing, hiking, and urban adventures. Each time we cooked together, I brought home new recipes to try on my own. Many became go-to family favorites, including her Strata, Mulligatawny Stew, and Baked Oatmeal. I relished my role as her sous-chef — and now I hear her voice offering tips and encouragement while I cook. I'm thrilled to have these special recipes in what I know will become my most-used cookbook.

Marianne's impact on me extended far beyond the kitchen. After becoming friends in college, we continued to strengthen our bond through frequent phone conversations, memorable visits and epic trips. She lived with zest, sought and seized opportunities for exploration and adventure, and infused every encounter with kindness and connection.

Marianne's kitchen was part science lab and part artist's studio, a bustling place of experimentation and creativity. When she launched her 'Party Hands' catering business in 2004, to share her passion for seasonal, healthy cooking with others, I was an enthusiastic advisor. Her replies to my standard "what's cooking?" telephone queries became longer as she described the scrumptious feasts she created featuring the freshly harvested Central Valley produce she loved.

Cooking classes came next, in response to requests from catering clients and their guests. An inspiring teacher, Marianne encouraged her students to slow down and enjoy the process of creating delicious healthy meals, one taste at a time. Ingredients mattered to Marianne — the fresher the better! Her garden yielded abundant harvests and was a haven of growth and beauty. Marianne was a locavore before it was trendy. She gleaned kiwi and oranges from neighbor's trees, got house-calls from mushroom foragers, and enthusiastically sampled and shopped her way through farmers' markets and food festivals. She enthusiastically supported local growers and artisan food-makers, believing in the positive impact they have on our community, our environment, and our health. After discovering a delicious new ingredient, Marianne often tracked it to its source and developed a relationship with the grower/producer. She began buying in bulk for her own use and catering, which led to her huge decision to sell the products that she loved to others.

In 2010, 'Party Hands' morphed into 'Marianne's Pantry,' with an ever-expanding line of oils, vinegars, grains, beans, spices and specialty foods. Orders flowed in via her website, retail partners and tastings at community events. Perhaps you've swooned over her Lemon Olive Oil, Fig Balsamic Vinegar, or Porcini Mushroom Mix. A savvy entrepreneur, Marianne's passion for her products and attention to detail fueled her growing business. She enjoyed designing labels, sourcing sustainable packaging, creating fun gift sets, adding tips to her website, and experimenting with new recipes to share.

Publishing a cookbook was one of Marianne's lifelong dreams, and she was thrilled to look through a draft of Cooking With Marianne before she left us, way too soon. I'm grateful to Heidi Russell for kick-starting this project, to Marcia Repaci for her graphic design expertise, and to the love of Marianne's life, Dave, for being taster-extraordinaire and so much more. Deepest thanks from all of us to Bill and Chantal McCarroll for their fun, upbeat, creative, brilliant, nurturing daughter, and for underwriting publication of this special cookbook. It's a wonderful legacy from Marianne to all of us, and we'll honor her with each culinary creation that brings health and joy to our tables and our lives.

Lisa Merrill

APRIL 2016

Table of Contents

Table of Contents - continued

Table of Contents - continued

Table of Contents - continued

Table of Contents - *continued*

Marianne cooking at the "Low Table Café" with view of Cloud's Rest Peak, Yosemite National Park, California, 2012

Healthy Eating & Cooking Tips

Healthy Eating & Cooking Tips

Marianne was committed to improved personal and universal health through mindful eating and sustainable practices at every level. These were pillars in her world, at work and at home.

If you look closely at the ingredients in Marianne's recipes and notice what ISN'T there, you'll quickly see that she prized healthy whole foods direct from the source. These foods burst with flavor, and their lack of processing and excessive packaging treads lightly on our earth.

The next few pages include tenets and tips for healthy cooking and eating from www. MariannesPantry.com. Much more than a place to order delicious products, Marianne's website was not just a place to order delicious products, but was also a vibrant work of love and art, featuring recipes, menus, and informative articles for anyone seeking to cook and eat for a healthier body and a healthier world.

WATER

Drink 64 ounces, or more, of filtered water every day. Drink most of it between meals to keep it from diluting and interfering with the digestive process.

SODAS AND OTHER SWEETENED DRINKS

Eliminate them altogether, or at least cut down to an occasional treat. It's worth the effort to find deliciousness in a glass of water with a slice of cucumber, lime or orange, a sprig of mint or basil, or a splash of fruit juice. Or try a mug of herb tea with a bit of honey or organic sugar.

FRUIT

Eat fruit twice a day, every day. Eat whole fruit, rather than just drinking the juice. Much of fruit's goodness comes from its fiber, which does not always make it to the glass. Enjoy fruit as a snack between meals or after dinner instead of a rich dessert. Branch out and try new varieties, locally grown if possible.

VEGETABLES

Think "colors of the rainbow" on your plate every day. You want to look down and see twice as many vegetables as meat, rice, potatoes and pasta. If you had a bad experience with a vegetable five, ten, or thirty years ago, be brave and try it again!

Think "farm-to-table." Learn which vegetables are grown in or near your region during each season, and seek out merchants who sell fresh, locally grown produce. It is usually less expensive and much more flavorful. Farmers' markets are a wonderful way to meet local growers and get vegetables and fruit that are fresh-from-the-fields.

Incorporate raw vegetables into your daily diet – coleslaw, shredded carrot or broccoli salad, celery root remoulade, or perhaps a snack of sugar snap peas, celery and carrot sticks. Heat breaks down some of the biologically active nutrients in food, so don't overcook it.

Double or triple the amount of vegetables called for in meat soups, stews and curries. Be sure to have at least twice the weight of vegetables to meat, and add extra vegetables to pasta dishes.

VEGETABLES, STORING

Refrigerators cool by removing moisture from the air, which is why vegetables wilt if not stored in a plastic bag. But, if moisture is trapped in the bag with no layer to absorb it, it will cause the the vegetables to rot prematurely and get slimy. When you bring produce home, remove any tight ties that may be holding bunches together. Discard any slimy or discolored parts. Rinse with cool water and gently shake to remove any excess water. Place the greens into either a brown paper bag or loosely roll them in a linen towel, paper towel, or napkin. If the vegetables are very dry, sprinkle a few drops of cool water on the towel, and put the roll in a produce bag. There is no need to use a twist-tie to reseal the bag, as a little aire can be good. Store these packages carefully so they don't bruise or crush one another. Herbs that come in a clamshell package can be kept just as they are.

Big Flavor without Big Fat

Fats are essential to many bodily functions, and they are a slow burning source of energy, so some fat in every meal helps us to maintain that "full" feeling longer. Sadly, most Americans eat too much fat and they don't eat the kind that our bodies need. Hydrogenated and partially hydrogenated oils (the bad fats) are in most processed and fast foods.

Without any fat, food can't brown, caramelize, or get crispy. I find that 1 T of oil/butter is sufficient to sauté 3-4 cups (about a pound) of chopped vegetables.

Quality ingredients don't need as much fat. If you want meals with less fat, start by using fresh, top quality ingredients and get creative in your seasoning to make the flavors "pop." Here are a few ideas:

- **Citrus fruits - oranges, lemons, limes** - Use the juice and also the zest (the colored part of the peel) to brighten foods. To get more juice, warm the fruit 10-15 seconds in the microwave and/or roll the whole fruit with pressure across a cutting board before juicing.

- **Fresh Herbs** - another great way to add flavor without fat.

- **Spices** - get to know a few spices and start using them! A few big hitters are cumin, coriander, and garam masala (a blend from India).

- **Other Flavor Enhancers** - Fresh ginger, garlic, horseradish, soy, salsa, and chutneys add flavor and interest without adding a lot of calories.

Par-Cooking

Par-cooking refers to a process in which vegetables (or other foods) are partially cooked. This can be useful in a number of ways. For complicated meals or large crowds, par-cooking ingredients that take longer to cook can help you to control the timing of your meal preparation so that everything is ready to serve at the same time. It is also a great way to gently cook vegetables so they maintain their texture, color, and valuable nutrients. Par-cooked vegetables make a wonderful snack and can make a dinner come together more easily.

- In wide sauté pan, bring 1" of water to boil and add a little salt. Cut vegetables into like-sized pieces and add to boiling water, with the stem end up. You don't need to cover them completely.

- If you will be using vegetables for a crudité platter, boil for just 2-3 minutes. When cooking large pieces of broccoli or cauliflower, it might take 4-5 minutes. You want to just remove the hard crunch, but not cook them all the way. Use a slotted spoon to remove vegetables from boiling water and set them in a wide bowl with cold water and ice cubes. This will quickly stop the cooking and preserve their bright color. Remove from ice water when cool, and refrigerate.

- If you're eating the vegetables immediately, drain and toss them with a bit of butter or olive oil and fresh ground pepper. If you want the vegetables to have a dry glaze, cook for another 1-3 minutes.

- Save the cooking water to use as a light, nutritious stock for soups and rice dishes.

BREAD CRUMBS

There is no need to throw away those thick, crusty ends of a loaf of bread, or even the inner parts when they get a bit stale. Chop or tear good quality bread into pieces. Dry on a rimmed tray for 15-20 minutes in a 300 degree oven. Whirl in a food processor or blender to the desired texture. Season with salt, pepper, paprika, Parmesan cheese, and herbs, if desired.

BROTH / STOCK

Getting into the habit of making and freezing broth is akin to composting for a committed vegetable gardener. I make broth as I cook, and often freeze for future use. Sometimes it is the water that I par-cook vegetables in. Sometimes it is a full blown pot of vegetables with roasted meat bones. I usually supplement these broths with a spoon or more of a concentrated bouillon product like "Better Than Bouillon" to provide sodium and more depth of flavor. For more detailed preparation steps, see my recipes for homemade broth in the "Savory Soups" chapter.

HERBS & SPICES

An herb is the leafy green part of the plant. A spice is the seed, bark, hull or other non-leafy part.

1. Use fresh herbs whenever you can, but good quality dried herbs work in most situations.

2. 1 t of dried herb = 3 t of fresh herb.

3. When using dried herbs, always crumble them before adding to dishes to release more flavor. When using fresh, add whole sprigs and remove before serving, or finely chop them and toss in at the last minute to give a more intense flavor. Don't chop woody stems.

NUTS AND SEEDS

Toasting enhances the flavor of nuts. This can be done in several ways; the key is to not let them burn. Toast before chopping, so there are fewer "crumbs".

• Stove Top: Put pieces in a single layer in a skillet on medium heat. Stir every 30 seconds or so for about 2-4 minutes.

• Oven: Spread nuts or seeds in a single layer on a pie plate or rimmed cookie tray. Put in a cold oven set to 325 for 8 minutes as it heats. Turn oven off and leave nuts in for 5-8 more minutes.

SALT, PEPPER & SEASONING BASICS

1. When tasting as you cook, ask yourself, what does this need—salt, heat, sweet, acid, fat, or more time for things to meld?

2. Keep salt handy in a small bowl and add it a pinch at a time. I like to use French Grey sea salt.

3. Use a pepper grinder to get the best pepper flavor. Get to know your pepper grinder. Measure how much comes out per grind. I usually use 8 "double-grinds" (back and forth) per 2 pinches of salt. 25 double grinds nets me about ¼ teaspoon.

4. White pepper is black pepper that has had the hull removed. It is used when the black flecks of pepper would not add to the look of a dish - as in a white sauce or corn chowder.

5. Except in the case of a stock, stew or sauce that is to be reduced, add salt and pepper as you go along. This means, season the onions as they are cooking, season again when you add the next ingredient. As you add more ingredients, re-taste and re-season appropriately. Use restraint when adding salt—you can always add more later, and of course, many people need to restrict their sodium intake for health reasons.

LEGUME BASICS AND COOKING TIPS

Get to know and eat more legumes. They offer complex carbohydrates, protein, fiber and a variety of vitamins and minerals. They can be used in soups, stews, salads, burgers, pancakes, dips, casseroles, and as wonderful side dishes. Integrating legumes into your diet is a great first step. The next is transitioning from using canned beans to dried ones. I soak a cup or two of dry beans every week, without always having a definite plan for them. I trust that I'll find the perfect use for them by the time they are soaked and cooked. If not, I freeze the cooked legumes and use later.

What exactly are legumes? Basically, they develop their fruit (or seed) inside a pod. Sometimes we eat both the fruit (seeds) along with the pods, as in snap peas or yellow or green "string" beans.

Since the "seeds" of legumes can be dried and kept indefinitely, most of the wide variety of legumes are best known in their dry form, although many can also be obtained fresh, depending on what grows in your region. In Central California farmer's markets, we usually find fresh fava beans, black eyed peas, and cranberry beans during their season. As with tomatoes, "heirloom" varieties exist that were beloved 50-150 years ago. The appearance, flavor, and texture set these heirlooms apart and make them worth the search and extra cost.

COOKING FRESH LEGUMES

Fresh beans do not need to be soaked. Cook fresh shelled beans in simmering water or stock for 10-30 minutes until tender. Add them to soups and stews, serve as a warm side dish with some minced onion and garlic or make them into a salad.

SOAKING DRIED LEGUMES

Once dried, all legumes, except lentils and split peas, need to be soaked before cooking. Since dry beans are actually seeds, soaking them for a day or so essentially "sprouts" the seed. This makes the nutrients more available to our bodies, makes the cooked product easier to digest, and cuts down on cooking time.

THE SLOW SOAK

Cover beans with four times as much water. A one quart container is perfect for 1 cup dry beans. Let sit in a cool place (under 72° or they may ferment) for 4-8 hours. Then, cover and refrigerate up to 48 hours. A 12-16 hour soak is sufficient but longer is better, if possible.

THE QUICK SOAK

If you are pressed for time, bring the beans to a boil, boil for 1 minute, then turn the pan off and let them soak for one hour. Then proceed as below. I use this method on occasion, but I find that the skins soften better and the flavors develop more deeply with the slow soak.

COOKING DRIED LEGUMES

1. Drain and rinse the beans. Remember, these are farm products that may contain sticks, stones or clods of dirt - especially if they come direct from smaller growers.

2. Cook 1 cup dry beans in a 1.5 quart pan (2 cups in a 3 quart pan and so on) covered by 2-3 inches of water.

3. Bring beans to a boil, cover and adjust heat to a simmer. Skim off any foam with a slotted spoon. Once the foam subsides, add a couple cloves of garlic, bay leaves, a chunk of onion, a ham hock, or piece of fat back and/or a few sprigs of fresh herbs, if desired.

4. Cook mostly covered at a low boil. Check the beans for doneness according to package directions or check every 15 minutes after 45 minutes of cooking. Scoop up a few beans in a spoon and blow on them: if the skins start to peel off, they're done. Another test is to gently bite on a

bean. It should "give." Fresher beans and legumes that have soaked longer cook more quickly. Some beans that are really old or have been stored at high temperatures may split open but never really soften.

5. If the water seems to have disappeared, bring some to boil in a separate pan and add it.

6. Don't add lemon or tomato until they are cooked. The acid from these fruits interferes with the cooking process.

7. If some of the beans are falling apart and others don't seem to have softened, but they've been cooking for over an hour, stop cooking them by removing the pan from the heat and letting them cool in the pan. They should "even out" by the time they have cooled.

8. Once the beans are cooked, salt to taste. I start with ½ t sea salt per cup dry beans.

9. Refrigerate cooked beans once they have cooled.

10. Always save the bean cooking water. In some varieties, this "pot liquor" is as tasty as the beans! Use it to to thicken the bean sauce, or as soup stock.

ELEVATION AND BEANS

Legumes take much longer to cook at altitudes over 5000 feet, where water boils at a lower temperature. If you do cook at high altitudes, plan on doubling the time. Keep replenishing water as it boils off, and use a lid.

YIELDS

1. For most dry beans, ½ lb dry (1.25-1.3 cups) = 2 ½-3 cups cooked beans.

2. One 15 oz can = about 1⅓ cups cooked beans (½- ⅔ cups raw).

3. A pound of dry beans (2-2½ cups) yields 5-7 cups cooked beans, the equivalent of 3-5 15 oz cans. Not only do dry beans offer a cost savings, they are also a more sustainable choice; they take up less space on your pantry shelf and in the tractor trailer trucks on our highways. Additionally, you control the amount of sodium.

4. Fresh, in-the-shell-bean yields vary. You'll get 1 to 1.5 cups shelled beans per pound of beans in the pod. They don't expand much at all when cooked. Fresh beans are truly a labor of love, but the taste is so wonderful, I find myself using them whenever I can get them.

Bountiful Breakfasts

Pancakes-a-Plenty!

Pancakes are a breakfast favorite and there are so many possibile variations to keep them from getting boring, and make them more healthy at the same time. Batters can be changed and fruit and nuts can be added. Try a fruit sauce instead of maple syrup. They keep well in the refrigerator for a few days and reheat easily in a toaster, toaster oven or buttered skillet. Freeze them by placing pieces of wax or parchment paper between each pancake before putting in a plastic bag in the freezer.

Basic Multi-Grain

INGREDIENTS: *Makes 12 4" pancakes*

½ c white flour

½ c whole wheat flour

¾ c oats

¼ c flax seed meal

2 T sugar

2 ½ t baking powder

½ t baking soda

½ t salt

2 eggs

1 1/3 - 1 2/3 c milk; start with less; add more if needed.

Soy or almond milk can be used - may need less

2 T unsalted butter, melted

10-12 oz (2½ - 3 c) blueberries, 4 bananas or other fruit (optional)

3-4 t butter for griddle, 1 t at a time

VARIATIONS:

The following two batter variations call for different flours, leavening agents, and/or liquids. Beyond that, they use the same ingredient list as above, and all the pancake recipes follow the same basic preparation steps described on the following page.

White Flour

2 cs all-purpose unbleached white flour (replaces the flours, oats & flax seed meal in the multi-grain option)

1 ⅓ - 1 ½ c milk

Buttermilk Multigrain

Use 1 t baking powder

Use ½ t baking soda

Use ¼ t salt

Use 1 ⅔ c buttermilk (replaces other milks)

FRUIT IN PANCAKES

- Blueberries, blackberries, raspberries, bananas, strawberries, peaches, are all great options. Some people mix the fruit into the batter; some put it on the cooking pancakes. Either way works; the second can be pretty, but dirties the cooking surface & flipper.

MAKING A FRUIT SAUCE

- If you have a plethora of fruit, this is a great option. I used up seven heavenly garden peaches by putting them in the batter and a fruit sauce.

1-2 T butter

3-5 c fresh fruit

2-3 T brown sugar or honey

1/2+ t vanilla extract

½ t spice of choice, optional (cinnamon, ginger, cardamom, etc…)

- Small chop the fruit. Melt the butter in a small pot and add the fruit, sugar and vanilla. Cook on medium high 3-5 minutes, then turn down and simmer to get the texture you like. If the pieces seem too big; use a potato masher to smooth the texture.

BASIC PANCAKE PREPARATION:

• Use whisk or sifter to combine dry ingredients in large bowl.

• If using fruit, stir it gently into the dry ingredients tocoat each piece. Make a well in the center.

• In a separate bowl, lightly beat the eggs, then add milk and melted butter.

• Pour the liquid ingredients into the well you made in the dry. Use a fork to gently draw the dry into the wet. Only mix the batter until the lumps are almost gone and the fruit is mixed in.

• Let the batter rest as long as you can - 20 minutes to 2 hours. Stir as little as possible after this step.

• This is a good time to make the fruit sauce, if you plan to use some.

• When ready to cook, preheat the griddle or a heavy pan to 350 - 360º, and very lightly butter it.

• Using a ¼ cup measure, scoop to fill, minimally disturbing the rest of the batter. Pour onto the griddle, spacing cakes so they don't run together (too much).

• If using, warm the maple syrup, 2-4 T per person.

• When bubbles appear on the pancake surface and the undersides are golden, 3-4 minutes, turn and cook 2-3 minutes longer, until golden on the bottom.

A double batch of pumpkin pancakes on the griddle is perfect for an Autumn morning. Adding pureed pumpkin to the batter gives them a warm orange color, but any mashed winter squash can be used. Use a 1/4 cup measurer to spoon onto griddle.

Pumpkin Pancakes

INGREDIENTS: *Makes 26 - 4"cakes*

2 c flour; good to use ½ or more whole wheat

¼ c flax seed meal

4 T brown sugar

1 T baking powder

½ t baking soda

1 t cinnamon

1 t ginger

½ t nutmeg

½ t salt

1 c chopped nuts

2 eggs

2 c buttermilk

4 T butter, melted

1 15 oz can pumpkin puree (not pie filling!) OR

1 lb cooked mashed winter squash

1 ½ t butter for the griddle

Banana Pancakes

INGREDIENTS: *Makes 12 - 4" cakes*

2 c flour; good to use ½ or more whole wheat

1-2 T brown sugar

1.5 t baking powder

¼ t baking soda

1 t cinnamon

¼ t salt

½ c walnuts

2 ripe bananas

1 t fresh ginger, minced

1 egg

1 c buttermilk

1 t vanilla

2 T butter, melted

1.5 t butter for the griddle

Corn Pancakes

These pancakes would be wonderful as part of a brunch, but we always have them with dinner. They explode with the natural sweetness of corn from using some pureed, some whole, and corn meal, as well. Corn is an excellent source of fiber, antioxidants, Vitamin B6, potassium and protein. Most other recipes for corn pancakes add sugar and use a lot more butter. We like them prepared as below.

INGREDIENTS:

Makes 8 to 12 3- 4" pancakes (serves 4 as a side)
OR 20-24 appetizer sized cakes

½ c white flour

2 c cooked corn (about 3 ears). You may sub up to ½ c shredded zucchini, in a pinch

1/3 c milk

1/3 c flour

1/3 c corn meal

½ t each salt and fresh ground pepper

2 eggs, beaten

2 T melted butter

2 T yogurt, chevre cheese or more melted butter

PREPARATION:

• Put ½ the corn with the milk in a blender (you could blend all, but if you want the batter a little chunky, best to add half the corn later).

• Mix the dry ingredients in a bowl.

• Add the corn, and mix to combine. Add the eggs, yogurt and butter. Gently mix to combine.

• If you have one, heat electric griddle to 360 and lightly oil it.

• For 4" pancakes, use a slightly heaping ¼ cup measure.

• Adjust size as desired. Cook 4+ minutes each side. If the pancakes are golden but seem to stick, spray a little oil under the pancake while you flip them.

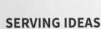

SERVING IDEAS

• Serve with caviar and sour cream or yogurt.

• Serve with a fresh mango or other salsa.

• Serve with butter and maple syrup.

TO REFRIGERATE OR FREEZE EXTRAS

• Stack cakes with pieces of wax paper (or saran) in between each. Wrap in foil to freeze. Freeze up to 2 months. Remove from freezer in the morning and let thaw in the refrigerator

TO REHEAT

• Pop into a toaster or toaster oven or reheat in a lightly oiled or buttered skillet.

Coconut Almond Granola

We eat fruit salad with yogurt topped with granola for breakfast most weekday mornings. The base recipe came from Robert Redford's Sundance Resort in Utah (worth a visit!). The coconut almond flavor combination came from granola we bought at Mana Foods in Paia, Maui. It's been 6-8 years and we still haven't tired of it!

INGREDIENTS: *Makes 5-6 cups, about 1.5-1.75 lbs*

- 1.5 c almonds or your choice chopped nuts/seeds
- 3 c rolled oats
- 2/3-1 c flax seed meal or wheat germ (optional)

- 1-1 ½ t cinnamon (or ginger/ allspice etc..)
- 2-3 T olive oil
- 1 ½ t vanilla extract

- 1/3 c honey or maple syrup or a combination
- 2 T molasses; can substitute one of above
- 1½ c medium shredded coconut

PREPARATION:

- Preheat oven to 275º.
- Toss first four ingredients in a large bowl. Chop some of the nuts as desired.
- Mix next four ingredients in a small saucepan and heat gently.
- Line a cookie tray with parchment paper.
- Pour the honey oil mixture into the oats bowl and toss thoroughly.
- Spread the mixture onto the parchment.
- After 12 minutes rotate the tray 180º and move to a higher or lower position in the oven.
- After 24 minutes, put the oats back in the bowl and mix in the coconut. Then put back on the tray and keep baking.
- After 36 minutes, rotate and change shelves one last time.
- After 48 minutes, check the granola. If all is golden, pull it out. If it doesn't seem cooked at all, rotate and give it 12+ minutes more. If it seems mostly cooked, rotate the pans, turn off the oven and leave the trays in for another 8-12 minutes.
- Once the granola is golden, remove it and cool completely. Store in jars or other airtight containers up to one month. It freezes well, too (see Cook's Notes).

* Adapted from an article about Sundance Resort in Utah.

COOK'S NOTES

- This recipe fills one large cookie tray. If you'll be eating as cereal, make a double or triple batch - or it will be gone really quick! Freeze extra in zip-lock storage bags.

- The trays have to be shuffled every 12 minutes, so have something else to do in the kitchen while this cooks.

- Use this recipe as a base template and make your own favorite flavors!

Fruit Crisps

We have found that eating homemade pies and crisps for breakfast gives us many of the food groups and gets the "sweet tooth thing" out of the way - when we have some self-control on portion size, that is.

I bake it at night along with dinner. That way it can rest and "gel" by morning. Crisp is like lasagna; cutting into it too soon ends up in a runnier experience. It is still yummy, but it is best if you can give it at least 40 minutes to rest before eating. This recipe makes a double batch — which I highly recommend.

TOPPING INGREDIENTS:

- Topping can be made ahead and refrigerate in a 1 quart resealable bag.

½ c very cold butter cut in little chunks

½ c brown sugar

1 c whole wheat flour (may substitute white flour)

½ t salt, if butter is unsalted

1½ t cinnamon or other spice as desired

1 c oats, preferably non-instant

TOPPING PREP:

- Combine butter through flour. This can be done in a food processor in seconds. Pour mixture into large bowl when it is mixed.

- **OR** wash hands and work butter in with fingers to make it like "play-dough" rather than "dusty". This takes a few minutes, but makes a better topping.

- Mix in oats, keeping the play-dough texture.

TOPPING FLAVOR IDEAS AND ADD-IN OPTIONS

- Substitute 1¼ t ginger for cinnamon on peaches

- Use all oats and no flour

- Add 1/3 c wheat germ, oat bran, flax seed

- Add ½ cup chopped nuts and/or coconut

- Reduce butter by half and add ⅔ cup shredded cheddar, with apples and pears.

 FILLING FOR RIPE STONE FRUIT, RIPE PEAR, BERRY CRISPS

1-2 T sugar per pound fruit

1 T cornstarch per lb fruit - can sub flour

1-2 t lemon juice per pound, optional

½ t lemon, orange zest per pound, optional

- Before doing anything, preheat oven to 350.

- Add above ingredients to the fruit. Mix gently but thoroughly.

- Lightly grease a 2-quart Pyrex or other pan, see pan size details below.

Fruit Crisps . . . *continued*

- Put fruit into pan, shaking to settle. Don't overfill or mound, as juices will overflow & burn.
- Spread topping evenly. Clump it with your hands for a streusel-like topping.
- Berries should take 30-45 minutes, soft stone fruits and pears 40-60 minutes. Check crisp at 15-20 minute intervals. If there is overflow, shove an old cookie tray or piece of foil on the lower rack to catch drips.
- Cool 30 minutes - overnight before serving.

 FILLING FOR APPLE, HARD PEAR, AND HARD STONE FRUIT CRISPS

2 T sugar per pound cut fruit

1 T flour per pound cut fruit

2 t lemon juice per pound cut fruit

Zest of ½ lemon or orange, optional

- Mix lemon juice and ½ the sugar with the fruit. Let rest 15-45 minutes, stirring every 5-10 minutes.
- When ready to cook, preheat oven to 375.
- If there is excess juice, pour half off and use to "baste" the crisp.
- Add the rest of the sugar, flour, zest and dried fruit if using. Transfer to buttered 2 quart dish, shaking to level fruit. Don't put the topping on yet. See pan size info below if needed.
- Cover with foil and bake 30 minutes.
- Uncover, and "baste" if desired. Now put on topping. Bake uncovered another 25-30 minutes.

COOK'S NOTES

- Crisp can be made ahead & reheated. Cook 10 minutes short of being done. Reheat 15+ minutes to serve. If it has been refrigerated, cover to warm - may take 30 minutes.

- Placement in the oven makes a difference. Things higher up in the oven will brown on top. Things bubble quicker and brown on the bottom when lower in the oven.

ABOUT FRUIT FILLINGS

- Soft fruits can liquefy if cooked higher than 350, so be careful.

- Use 3½-4 lbs fruit - you need 3+ lbs chopped, but you lose some from pits, bruises, apple peels etc.

- You can replace one pound of fresh fruit with 12 oz dried fruit. Lightly dried Bing cherries are a great choice!

- You can use more apples, but too much soft fruit may cause overflow.

- Chop fruit into same size pieces. 1/8 -1/16th inch wedges are good.

- Peach-blueberry, peach-cherry, nectarine-plum, pear-dried cranberry, apple-blackberry, apple-raisin - the sky's the limit!

Breakfast Risotto with Almonds & Dried Cherries

This recipe can be enjoyed with einkorn farro instead of the rice and it will be even better for you! Follow the proportions described below, replacing einkorn for rice, and cook for 40-50 minutes total.

INGREDIENTS:

Makes 4+ cups, 4+ servings

1 c carnaroli rice

2½ c water

1 T butter or mild olive oil

¼+ t cinnamon or other spice

¼ t salt

½ t vanilla or almond extract

2-3 T brown sugar - less if sweetened milk

2-2½ c almond, soy or regular milk

1 c dried cherries

¼ c almonds, toasted and chopped

PREPARATION:

• Combine rice, water, butter, cinnamon and salt in a 3 quart pot.

• Bring to a simmer and cook 20 minutes at a solid simmer, stirring every 3-5 minutes.

• Add 1 cup almond milk and the cherries. Stir in gently.

• Cook another 3-5 minutes. Stir in brown sugar to taste and add 2/3 of the nuts.

• Add more milk as needed.

• Sprinkle on more nuts at serving. Pour on extra milk or a pat of butter, as desired.

• After serving, sprinkle remaining nuts onto remaining risotto and store covered in the refrigerator for another delicious breakfast.

COOK'S NOTES

• Like oatmeal, this makes a delicious rib-sticking breakfast.

• Experiment with the flavors, using other nuts or fruits, as desired.

• Enjoy for several mornings as single portions reheat easily in the microwave. Just add milk to bring it to your desired consistency.

Marianne in Canyonlands National Park, Utah, 2009

Baked Oatmeal

Everyone who has had this hot, creamy and fulfilling breakfast dish gives it a big thumbs up! It is great on a cold winter morning. Putting it together the night before makes it easy for everyone to enjoy a hot breakfast together, no matter how big the crowd.

COOK'S NOTES

• Once cooked, this keeps several days. Reheat pieces in the toaster oven or microwave.

• Baking temp is flexible 325-375—less time if oven is hotter.

• Use more sugar, eggs, or butter, as desired.

• Steel cut oats can replace 1 cup of the oats. Add 1½ cups more milk. You will need a larger pan (or split in two).

• Fruit options are totally flexible, fresh or frozen will work; blueberries, peaches, mangoes, etc... can replace both fresh and dried fruits.

• Try cherries (dry or fresh), nectarines, dried cranberries, persimmon, raisins, or dates.

• Apricots seemed too dry. Try soaking them in sherry first.

• 10 dried peach halves +1 t (or more) fresh ginger.

INGREDIENTS:

Makes 2 quart baking dish - 6 large, 8 med servings

2 c regular (not quick) oats

1 ½ t baking powder

½ t ground cinnamon

½ t salt

½ c chopped nuts

¾ c chopped dried fruit

1 large (8-10 oz) apple or pear, finely chopped, shredded or mashed - or applesauce

2-4 large eggs, beaten (more if big exercise day)

⅓ c brown sugar

2 T melted butter

3½ c milk -Can use soy or almond milk

PREPARATION:

• Set oven to 350 degrees (325-375 as needed) if baking immediately.

• Combine first six ingredients.

• Combine other ingredients in a separate bowl and stir well.

• Add to oat mixture.

• At this point, the batter can be refrigerated overnight, if preferred. Refrigerate in the mixing bowl, the greased baking pan (it will fill a two quart pan to the top), or a resealable bag.

• Bake 40-50 minutes.

• **Note:** It also works fine to put the pan in the oven right when you turn it on.

Mexico Memories

Marianne explored the colonial cities of San Miguel de Allende and Guanajuato with Lisa Merrill in 2010. Each day brought new opportunities to learn, connect, and enjoy the regional cuisine.

▼ *Buying beans from street vendor*

▼ *Enjoying views from roof of Bed & Breakfast*

▼ *Day of the Dead celebration*

► *Fresh-cooked tlacoyos (toasted corn cakes) at outdoor market*

► *Traditional snack of jicama spiced with chili powder*

▲ *Daily stop for fresh-squeezed orange juice*

Savory Soups

Homemade Vegetable Broth

When I'm using a lot of vegetables and will be in the kitchen for a while, I start a pot of this on the back burner. Also, if I know I'll be making broth, I save up vegetable scraps for a day or two, cleaned and refrigerated.

EQUIPMENT NEEDED

- 4-8 quart stock pot with lid
- Skimmer utensil—small fine-mesh strainer or Chinese type fryer spoon or basket
- Potato masher or large wooden spoon
- Large colander (preferably metal with holes)
- A second large pot or big mixing bowl

BASIC INGREDIENTS

3-4 quarts water

¼ to 1 cup white cooking wines (combine unfinished bottles and keep in fridge)

1 large onion with skin, coarsely chopped

3-4 cloves unpeeled garlic

2+ stalks celery chopped in 2" pieces - leaves ok

2+ carrots chopped in 2" pieces

½ lemon, orange, or lime with rind cut in 3 pieces

12-20 peppercorns (same of whole coriander, mustard, fennel, cloves and other aromatic spices if available—2 to 4 kinds are fine)

3-5 sprigs each of various fresh herbs

1 t salt (you will salt more when you use broth)

EXTRA INGREDIENTS AS AVAILABLE

vegetable ends/peelings/skins from tomato, apple, or potato

broccoli ends, cauliflower leaves

corn cobs

PREPARATION

- Combine and heat the Basic Ingredients. Cover the pan until it comes to a boil and then keep it partially covered. You want to achieve a steady, gentle boil throughout.
- Add Extra Ingredients to the pot as you chop them.
- Skim off foam as it appears, then push/mash vegetables into water.
- Add water if needed to keep it all just covered.
- Keep the pot partially covered—this will slow the evaporation while flavors meld.
- Boil down until there is discernible flavor and color—don't expect more than 4-8 cups.
- Since it is not fully salted it may taste weak, but when you use it and salt it, it will perk right up.
- Once you want to call it done (1+ hour of boiling), let the stock cool so you don't burn yourself in the next step.
- Set the second stock pot or bowl in a clean sink and put the colander on top. Be sure nothing is angled or you'll have a mess!

continued on next page . . .

"VITAMIN WATER" FROM COOKING VEGETABLES

• Vegetables lose some of their valuable vitamins when steamed, boiled, or soaked in hot water. I save all remaining water from cooking and rehydrating vegetables. The only exception is stinky cauliflower or Brussels sprout water. I save only a small amount of this kind.

• Let the cooking water cool and then pour it into a storage container. Label the container and freeze. Keep adding liquid (and adding to the label) until the container is full.

• I use this "vitamin water" to start Basic Vegetable Broth and for cooking rice and other grains.

• If I need to use it as broth, I add a teaspoon or so of a bouillon base per quart —no more or it gets "fake" tasting.

• Carefully and gradually pour the mixture into the colander. If things get too full, stop. Empty the liquid into storage containers. I use quart size deli or yogurt containers. Push on the solids to give off their liquid, and then discard them.

• After the hard work, don't rush this part and have it spill down the drain.

• If you spill, join the club—just try not to do it twice.

• Resume the straining.

• Label the containers on the lid (masking tape and a Sharpie pen work great) and refrigerate 2-5 days or freeze.

ENHANCED BROTH—ADDING ROASTED BONES

Adding roasted bones to a simmering stock is standard procedure in top restaurant kitchens. Here's how to do it.

• As bones come into your life, put them into a heavy plastic bag and store in the freezer for future use.

• Preheat the oven to 375.

• Line a pan with parchment, put the bones on it and lightly oil and season them. Roast 45-75 minutes, turning twice, until they are fragrant and golden.

• Bones can be roasted a day or two ahead and stored covered in the refrigerator.

• Add bones to stock anytime. Cook 45-60 minutes.

• If you are short on time, unroasted bones will still work to enhance a stock.

Meat Stocks

Poaching any meat yields two things – a rich stock plus flavorful, moist cooked meat. A poach is NOT a boil. Barely bubbling is the goal. Plan to poach your meat a day or several hours ahead as the cooling time (2 hours) is a key part of preparing a meat stock.

 ## Poultry

- Start preparing the Basic Vegetable Broth, but use just 3 quarts water per whole chicken.

- Also add 1 t sea salt or to taste.

- Boil gently about 20 minutes, skim off the foam as it appears and push veggies down.

- Meanwhile, rinse, pat dry, quarter and mostly skin the chicken. After the 20 minutes, gently push in the pieces (discard skin) plus contents of the organ bag. Push the meat under the vegetables so it is covered.

- Partly cover and boil very gently for 30 minutes.

- Turn off and let rest covered for 1 hour.

- Uncover, put in a cool place, and let cool until you can handle the meat.

- Don't be in too much of a rush. The slow cool lets the meat shred more easily. And shredded meat really does taste better!

- Once cool, pick the meat off the bones in large hunks. Put in a container that just holds it and surround it with broth. Refrigerate until the meat is needed. Shred it at that time.

- Save the bones to roast and add to a future stock or discard.

- Strain and save the remaining broth in storage containers. Label the lid and refrigerate 2-5 days or freeze.

 ## Beef & Pork

This is one way to cook beef and pork for carnitas and other Mexican dishes.

- The process is the same as for poultry; make a broth with a variety of vegetables and spices and let that cook a while.

- Add meat, cover, and gently boil until it is almost falling apart.

- Let the meat cool in the pan and proceed as with poultry.

 ## Fish

This method makes the best base for a fish soup, stew, or chowder ever!

- Use a whole fish carcass that you have hacked into pieces. Clean it well of blood and cut out the gills.

- Start preparing the Basic Vegetable Broth, but use just 3 quarts water. Add more if needed to cover the fish.

- Don't use more than a smidge of any really strong vegetables—cabbage, broccoli, cauliflower, kale, Brussels sprouts. It could overpower the fish stock.

Carrot Ginger Soup

I first made this soup with carrots from two local farmers and it was a huge hit. Try to use freshly picked carrots, if possible. It really makes a difference. If you don't think you like ginger, you can leave it out — but please don't. This soup is wonderful and it freezes great, too!

INGREDIENTS

Makes 5-6 or so quarts

This can be made in a 6 quart pot, but it's too much to use an immersion blender.

4 T butter

1 huge (14 oz) onion, chopped

pinch of salt and red pepper flakes (will add more later)

3 T minced ginger

3 T minced garlic

4 lbs carrots with tops (so you know they're fresh)

1 cup almonds or cashews

2 T honey or agave nectar

1+ T salt

1 t white pepper, may sub freshly ground black

1 t turmeric

2 quarts broth, preferably homemade

2 cups cooked white beans, optional

1 quart buttermilk, 2 percent or whole

dash or three of sweet sherry just before serving, optional

4 ears corn and their cooking water, about 1 lb shucked, optional

PREPARATION

• If you're including corn, shuck it and heat about ½" water to boil in a 6 or 8 quart stock pot. Throw a pinch of sugar in the pot. Cook the corn for 3-4 minutes. Remove and wrap with a damp linen towel and let corn cool. Save the cooking water for the soup.

• Gently warm the butter in the same pot. Add the onions and cook at a heat that makes a little noise but won't burn the butter. When the onions start to soften, about 5 minutes, add a pinch of salt, 2 pinches of pepper flakes, the ginger, and garlic. Cook another 5 minutes or so.

• Chop the carrots coarsely and add, once the sauté is well softened. Also add the nuts, honey, 1 t salt, ¼ t pepper, and turmeric. Cook 3-4 minutes, stirring often. Salt and pepper the mixture to taste and cook 2 more minutes.

• Add the broth and bring to a boil. If broth is unsalted, taste and season as needed, but don't over salt. Once the soup boils, partially cover and reduce heat to maintain a simmer. Cook until the carrots are tender, 25-40 minutes. If using, add the corn or white beans after 15 minutes.

• Puree the soup using an immersion or regular blender. If using a regular blender, let the soup cool and carefully purée it in batches. If you want it really smooth, put through a strainer, tamis, or Chinese hat.

• As you are puréeing, add in the buttermilk. Taste and adjust seasonings to your liking.

• The soup tends to thicken, so don't hesitate to add more buttermilk, broth or milk to suit your taste.

• Sprinkle with sherry at serving.

Beef, Beet, and Cabbage Soup

Make this for vegetarians and use farro instead of beef. This freezes great! This is my compilation of several recipes. It has lots of vegetables and lots of seasonings. The apple juice makes it sweet, the garlic gives it bite, the lemon gives it tang. . . a symphony made with simple, common ingredients!

TO CHOP CABBAGE

Quarter the cabbage top to bottom. Cut out the hard white core. Cut each quarter into thirds top to bottom. Then slice thinly crosswise.

INGREDIENTS: *Makes about 5-6 quarts*

2 lbs beef short ribs or stew meat OR 1 cup emmer farro for a non-meat version

1½-1¾ lbs beets

salt and pepper

olive oil to brown

20 oz red onion, small chop (white OK in a pinch)

4 cloves garlic, thinly sliced

Plus several whole cloves of garlic

8 whole allspice berries

1 carrot, chunked

4-5 celery stalks or ¾ c peeled, chopped celery

4 cups apple juice, cider, or water

OR 16 oz organic diced tomatoes and 2 cups water or broth

2 cups water

4-8 cups good broth; do use some the beet cooking water

salt and pepper

1 lb. potatoes

1¼-1½ lbs. red or green cabbage

2 t dry dill

8-10 large garlic cloves, crushed

Juice of ½ lemon, or more to taste

1 bunch fresh dill, roughly chopped

1 bunch scallions, finely cut

2-3 t sea salt, to taste

1+ t fresh ground black or sweet red pepper, to taste

3 T finely chopped parsley, optional

Sour cream for garnish (1-2 T per bowl)

Cider or red wine vinegar for the table

PREPARATION

- If using ribs, salt them and, if you have time, let sit overnight in the refrigerator. Or just proceed.

- Brown the meat; dry meat thoroughly. Cut stew meat into small pieces. Rub with olive oil. Heat a heavy-bottomed pan and brown ½ in a single layer 5-6 minutes on one side. Salt and pepper then turn each piece with tongs and cook another 4-6 minutes. Repeat with the rest.

- Get beets cooking in a pan they just fit into in a single layer. Add water just to cover. Cover the pan and gently boil until beets are tender, 25-65 minutes. Save cooking water for the soup. Cool, peel, and shred or julienne. This can be done up to 2 days ahead.

- Get farro cooking if using. Directions below.

- Remove meat from pan; add the onions and garlic and brown. Season with salt and pepper. Remove ¾ of the onions.

- Start simmering the soup. Put the allspice and cloves in a tea or spice holder. Add to the pot with the cooked meat, carrot, celery, apple juice, and water. Simmer ½-1 ½ hours, or until meat is tender or just about falling off the bone.

- Cube potatoes and add along with 6-8 more cups of broth. Simmer 10 minutes. Thinly slice cabbage (see sidebar) and add with the beets, reserved onions, tomatoes, and emmer, if using, and dry dill.

- Once the cabbage starts to get limp, stir in the garlic, lemon juice, ½ the fresh dill, and the scallions. Remove from heat. Adjust seasonings to taste. It should need salt and pepper.

- Serve topped with sour cream and parsley or dill. Pass the pepper grinder and cider vinegar.

Cream of Celery Soup

Isn't it interesting how certain tastes and smells can trigger specific past memories? I first enjoyed this soup after spending a cold, clear day seeing and learning the fabulous history of Great Falls, Montana. I ended the day with this soup and hot cheese onion biscuits. Mmmm! It would also be great with a grilled bacon/cheese/tomato sandwich. If you peeled and cored an apple, I'll bet it would make a nice addition.

INGREDIENTS

Makes about 5 quarts

2½ lbs potatoes

3 lbs celery

8 cups water

1 t salt

1 T chicken bouillon base
(or 1½ t more salt)

1+ T butter

4 oz fine chopped prosciutto, optional

12 oz minced onion

¾ t celery seed

½ t sea salt

4 cups milk

¼ t dry mustard powder, or 1 t prepared mustard

¼ t white pepper

sea salt and black pepper, as needed

PREPARATION

• Rinse and chop the potatoes and celery into ¾" chunks.

• Set aside ½ lb celery to mince for garnish.

• Combine the chunks with the water, salt, and bouillon base in a 6+ quart soup pot. The water will not cover the vegetables.

• Bring to a boil and adjust temperature to a simmer, cover and cook until the vegetables are tender, 18-25 minutes.

• Mince the prosciutto, if using, and sauté in a little butter. Stir and adjust temperature and cook 4-7 minutes until it is nice and crisp. Remove to a small holding bowl.

• Mince the remaining celery and the onion. Sauté them in the same pan with a little more butter over medium heat. Add the seasonings after about 5 minutes. Continue to cook until they are soft and lightly colored, 10-12 minutes total.

• When the simmering vegetables are cooked, remove from heat and let cool 10-15 minutes before puréeing. Carefully transfer the vegetables, a few cups at a time, to a blender or food processor and puree until as smooth as desired. This may take a few batches. Or use an immersion blender.

• Return the purée to the soup pot and add the sauté as well as the milk and spices. Bring it back to a simmer for 5-8 minutes.

• Taste well and adjust seasonings as needed.

Cauliflower Apple Soup – Creamed & Curried

The apples add a touch of sweetness to this rich and flavorful soup. It is packed with healthy ingredients and hearty enough to make a full meal along with a good salad. Enjoy it while the weather is cool!

SOUP INGREDIENTS

Makes 5-6 quarts

6-8 cups not too salty stock (water and 1½-2 T bouillon concentrate is fine), at a boil

1+ T butter

3 cups onions, chopped (they'll get blended)

6 t Madras curry powder (2 t hot)

1½ t saffron threads or 6 pinches powder, optional

Sea salt and fresh ground black pepper to taste

3 apples, peeled, cored and chunked (+3 for dice)

3 lb cauliflower

24 oz russet potatoes, peeled and chunked

1- 2½ cups whole milk (or part ½-and-½)

3 T minced chives or parsley for garnish

1 T yogurt or sour cream per serving, optional

Sea salt and freshly ground black pepper to taste

CURRIED APPLE DICE INGREDIENTS

This cooks down a lot!

1 c apple juice or cider

3-4 apples, peeled, split, cored, cut in ¼-inch dice

1 T butter

1 t garam masala

¾ t saffron threads or 3 pinches powder, optional

Sea salt and freshly ground black pepper to taste

1+ lb fresh shrimp or lobster meat, optional

COOK'S NOTES

• This soup can be made into a complete meal by adding slices of cooked lobster or shrimp.

• Also great as a full meal with broiled blue cheese toasts and a frissée salad with hard-boiled egg.

• The broth and milk quantities are vague. Use less, rather than more, of both. But the soup thickens as it sits, so you may need it for the next day . . .

EQUIPMENT NEEDED

• Immersion or regular blender

continued on next page . . .

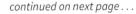

SOUP PREPARATION

- Melt the butter in an 8-quart stew pot over medium heat. Add the onions, curry powder, saffron, ½ t sea salt, ¼ t black pepper and sauté 3 minutes, stirring often.

- Add the sliced apple and sauté another 5 minutes, stirring often.

- Break up the cauliflowe. All parts except leaves can be used. Peel and dice the potatoes.

- Add the cauliflower, potatoes, and 7 cups of the chicken stock. The amount should not quite cover it. Cover and bring to a gentle boil.

- Boil until the vegetables are tender, about 20 minutes. Make the curry apple dice (see below) while waiting.

- When the soup vegetables are soft and cooked, turn off heat and blend thoroughly using an immersion blender. Or do carefully in a blender (hot! careful!). Add the milk as you blend it.

- Stir in half the curried apples and bring the soup back to below a simmer. If needed, thicken the soup by barely boiling it for 5-15 minutes. Season to taste with more salt, pepper, and curry powder.

- Serve garnished with yogurt and chives if desired, plus the rest of the apple dice.

SUBSTITUTION, MODIFICATION OPTIONS

- Use leeks for the onions.

- Use buttermilk for the milk—just don't boil it.

- If needed, add a teaspoon of honey or maple syrup.

- Use some or all winter squash chunks or pumpkin purée for the potato.

DRIED APPLE CHIPS

- Slice a whole apple very thin.

- Place the slices on a parchment-lined tray and dry in a 250 degree oven for 15-20 minutes, or until done.

- Garnish soup with apple chips at serving.

CURRY APPLE DICE PREP

- In a wide sauté pan, bring the cider (juice) to a boil and cook down to ¼.

- As cider reduces, slice apples thin and thumbnail size. If shrimp are large, slice into thick "coins." If small, leave whole.

- Once the juice is syrupy and down to ¼, add the apples, butter, and garam masala.

- Cook to soften and color, 3-4 minutes. Once soft, add the shrimp and cook briskly 2-3 minutes.

- Once everything looks shiny and coated, turn off.

Broccoli Cheese Soup

I first made this after picking up a magnificent 5¼ lb broccoli Romanesco. The soup is also wonderful made with traditional broccoli. You can also use part mushrooms and part broccoli, but it loses some of its pretty green color that way. Sauté the mushrooms before puréeing them. Swiss cheese is a great addition!

INGREDIENTS

Makes 5-6 quarts

1¼ lbs. potatoes

3 lbs. broccoli

10 cups broth or use less broth and more milk

2½ t salt if broth is unsalted

4-7 leeks or 20 oz onion; 2 huge or 3-4 large

3-5 ribs celery, about 1½ cups very thinly sliced

2 T butter or olive oil

Sea salt and lots of fresh ground pepper

4 cups milk, some half-and-half as desired

8 oz sharp Cheddar or Swiss cheese

OPTIONAL TOPPINGS / ACCOMPANIMENTS

• chopped scallions or chives (1 T per bowl)

• cooked, crumbled bacon

• toasted brown bread with cream cheese and chutney

PREPARATION

• Scrub potatoes. Peel, if you like, but I do so only sparingly because the skins contain a lot of nutrients. Chop into like-sized pieces and put in a stock pot with 2 quarts light broth.

• Add 1 t sea salt per quart broth if it's unsalted. Cover, bring to a boil, and simmer.

• While the potatoes cook, separate broccoli. Discard any woody stems and peel off any tough outer skin. Chop into like-sized pieces. Keep floret tops separate. Add stems to the potatoes after 10 minutes. If needed, add the remaining 2 cups broth to just cover everything. Salt to taste.

• Cook another 5-8 minutes or until everything is just softened, not mush.

• As the broccoli cooks, clean, chop and sauté leeks and celery in butter for 7-10 minutes.

• Salt and pepper as they cook. No need to brown, just soften and maintain bright colors.

• When broccoli and potatoes are cooked, remove from broth to a large bowl or pot along with half the broth. You'll purée this.

• Bring remaining broth back to a boil. Add florets and cook 3-4 minutes just until still bright and barely soft. Set aside about 6 cups of them in a strainer to cool. These will go in the puréed soup.

• Start puréeing the other cooked parts in batches; the florets, the sauté, the potatoes and broccoli. Add broth as needed to reach desired consistency. Clean the original pot and put the purée back into it. Add the milk and broth and heat gently.

• Grate in cheese and add remaining florets. Season to your preference.

Better than Memories Tomato Soup

When paired with "cheesed-up" crusty whole-grain bread, this soup is soul-and-belly-satisfying! Plus, it is easy to make, and if you have a surplus of fresh tomatoes from your garden, it is a great way to use up a bunch of them.

INGREDIENTS

2-3 large or 6-8 small leeks

4 t minced garlic

2 T butter

4 lbs. tomatoes

5-6 cups vegetable broth, preferably homemade

1 ½ cups dry white wine

6 T tomato paste, optional

2-3 roasted red peppers (can use rinsed, jarred)

2 cups cooked, seasoned white beans, optional (can use canned)

6 sprigs fresh basil

6 sprigs fresh parsley, optional

3 sprigs fresh thyme (or 2 t dry)

½ cup half-and-half

2 t salt, to taste

½-¾ t freshly ground black pepper

AT SERVING

1 cup shredded/small-cubed cheese of your choice

2 large slices whole-grain bread per person

cheese slices to melt on the bread

PREPARATION

- Clean and chop white parts of leeks to make 3-5 cups. Extra is OK.

- In a 6 quart pot, sauté leeks over medium heat in the butter, keeping the flame low enough not to brown them. Salt and pepper as they soften and add the garlic.

- Core and coarsely chop the tomatoes. Add them to the pan once the leeks are cooked.

- Also add 5 cups of the broth, the wine, paste, peppers, white beans, herbs, and half-and-half.

- Bring to boil. Adjust heat, simmer gently for an hour, stir often.

- Carefully pull out herb sprigs. Purée with immersion blender or in a blender. Let soup cool if using a regular blender.

- Taste and season to taste. Soup may need as much as 2 t salt.

- If soup seems too thick, add some of the remaining broth, water, or milk.

TO SERVE

- Heat oven to 350 and put slices of multigrain bread in for about 10 minutes, flipping after 5 minutes.

- Once they feel crispy, put the sliced cheese on and let it melt.

- Put the hot soup in bowls and stir in the shredded/cubed cheese.

- Serve the soup with the cheese toasts and plan to dip them into the soup as you eat and remember why everyone loved that canned soup as a kid!

Corn Chowder with Smoked Salmon or other Seafood

Use fresh, direct from the farm or garden, yellow corn in this chowder to give it this wonderful yellow color. This freezes great, so make extra for a cold winter night!

INGREDIENTS

Makes 4-6 quarts, about 12-15 servings

5-8 ears corn, or 5-6 cups kernels, or 2 lbs

1 lb green zucchini or string beans, optional

1 lb freshly pulled carrots, optional

2 lbs small red potatoes

2 cups rich vegetable cooking water

1+ lb smoked salmon, cooked crab meat, popcorn shrimp, or lobster meat, optional

6 - 8 cups 2% or whole milk

1 cup half-and-half, optional (or more milk)

2-3 t sea salt

1+ t white pepper

½ cup chopped fresh chives, dried won't do
  OR ½ cup very thinly sliced tops of green onions

PREPARATION

• In a 6-8 quart pot, bring 2" of water to boil. Add 1 t sugar and the husked corn—cut off any long stems so it will fit. Cover and cook 4-6 minutes after the water resumes boiling.

• Remove corn, leaving the water in the pot. Cool corn on a plate or in a lasagna type pan covered with a moist towel or cloth napkin. While corn cools, cook the rest of the vegetables.

• Small chop the potatoes and cook in the reserved corn water, covered and gently boiling until just tender, 10-14 minutes. Remove from water and put in a colander or pie plate to cool. Leave the water in the pot.

• Chop zucchini into small bite size and gently boil, covered, in the vegetable water 3 minutes until just tender.

• Remove from water to bowl. Leave the water in the pot.

• Boil down the vegetable water so there is no more than 2 cups and put in a small container.

• Rinse the pot and return it to the stove.

• Once the corn is cool enough to handle, cut kernels off cobs.

• Purée 4 cups of corn (about ⅔ of it) with 2-3 cups of the milk.

• Put back into the soup pot and cook gently.

COOK'S NOTES

• This can all be done in one pot if desired. Use a 6 or 8 quart pot from the start.

• Don't fret about having exact amounts of the vegetables. Just be sure every ingredient is fresh and delicious, or omit it.

• A blender is needed.

• The soup thickens as it sits, so it may need a little more broth or milk the next day.

• Sprinkle extra cut chives into the pot of chowder once it has cooled.

• The corn can be cooked and cut off the cobs up to 2 days ahead. Save the water you cooked the corn in and boil the bare cobs in it. Add water, if needed. Cover and cook 30-40 minutes for a FANTASTIC stock! Use this to cook the other vegetables too.

continued on next page . . .

Corn Chowder preparation continued . . .

- Add the broth, half-and-half, if using, and 2-3 more cups of the milk. Heat through.

- Add the rest of the corn and other vegetables as they are ready.

- Shred salmon, if using, and add along with salt and pepper. Add any seafood being used at this time.

- Stir soup gently so as not to break vegetables.

- It's OK if the soup accidentally boils, but keep the flame low AND stir so the bottom doesn't burn.

- Add 1 more cup milk if it fits into pan and taste to check seasonings. If there is room, and soup seems too thick, add the remaining milk.

AT SERVING

- Stir gently but well as goodies are in the bottom.

- Sprinkle each bowl with 1-2 t fresh chopped chives.

- Serve with herb biscuits and an heirloom tomato or green bean salad if it is summer and the produce is fresh!

Cold Cucumber Soup with Cubanelle Peppers and Nuts

SOUP INGREDIENTS

Makes about 6 cups; 4-6 servings

3 lbs flavorful Armenian, Persian, or English cucumbers

6-8 oz green Cubanelle or sweet Italian frying peppers (could be 4-6 small or 2 large—no bells!)

⅔ cup tangy green grapes from someone's arbor, optional

1 large garlic clove, chopped

¼ cup extra-virgin olive oil

½ cup unsalted roasted cashews, peanuts or pine nuts

2 T red wine vinegar

¾ t sea salt

¼ t white pepper; may sub freshly ground black pepper

½-1 cup water or light vegetable cooking water

Chopped chives or parsley at serving

Crispy herb bread crumbs at serving, optional (recipe at right)

SOUP PREPARATION

- Peel cucumbers, remove any really large seed bands and coarsely chop. Seed and coarsely chop the pepper.

- Purée everything in blender, adding water only if needed. Do in 2 batches. Puree as thoroughly as you desire.

- Transfer to a wide leftover container or bowl. Chill or freeze until cold, about 2 hours. Whisk before serving and add water and adjust seasonings to taste.

- Serve with chives and bread crumbs.

CRISPY HERB BREAD CRUMBS

This can be made ahead or while the soup cools.

2 slices multigrain bread or ½ cup panko bread crumbs

2 T fresh herbs, minced

pinch sea salt

a few grinds freshly ground pepper

good quality fresh olive oil

BREAD CRUMB PREP

- Toast bread/panko to golden in a toaster or skillet.

- If bread, tear into pieces. Pulverize to small bits/large crumbs in food processor or blender.

- Toast either in a dry skillet for 3-5 minutes to turn golden.

- Add 1+ t olive oil, salt, pepper, minced herbs. Toast 2 more minutes.

- Garnish each soup serving with a small spoonful.

Mushroom Wild Rice Soup with Chicken

This is my take on combining both chicken-rice and cream of mushroom soup. There are many different varieties of mushrooms available these days, either fresh or dried. It is fun to try some of the various shapes, sizes, and flavors. Mushrooms provide protein, fiber, nutrients, and minerals. Some even have medicinal values such as stimulating the immune system, and anti-inflammatory and anti-histimine properties.

This soup can easily be modified for vegetarians by eliminating the chicken and will still be wonderful. If you go that route, and want some extra protein, try adding some garbanzo beans. Always use good broth — it makes a difference!

INGREDIENTS

Makes 4-5 quarts

• Chicken needs to be poached and chilled. This can be done up to 2 days ahead.

• Rice can also be made ahead.

½ c wild rice

½ c brown rice

4 oz dried or 24 oz fresh mushrooms (or a combination)

2+ T butter (or chicken fat from broth if any)

6 oz finely chopped onion

8 oz leek (2 med/lg) or more onion

6 oz celery (3 lg stalks)

6 oz carrots

1 c sherry

10 cups good broth (store-bought low sodium is fine)

½ poached chicken (or rotisserie chicken)

½ t dry mustard

½-1 t tarragon

2-4 T butter

4 T flour

4 cups milk

OPTIONAL INGREDIENTS

1½-3 cups cooked garbanzo beans

¾ - 1½ lb peeled, cubed, cooked winter squash

12 oz small-chopped greens

preparation steps on next page . . .

PREPARATION

THE RICE

- In a 1½-2 quart saucepan, bring 2¼ cups water to a boil. Add ½ t salt. Turn off heat and add wild rice. Let sit.

- After 30 minutes, add the brown rice and simmer covered, about 50 minutes. Once rice is cooked, turn off heat, fluff rice with a fork, and let rest 10+ minutes uncovered.

THE SOUP

- Hydrate dry mushrooms if using. (See below).

- Sauté vegetables as described here. Or follow the shortcut option (see below)

- Start with onions and leeks, salting and peppering once they soften.

- Chop 1/3 of the celery into tiny pieces and add to the softening/browning onions.

- If things get dry, turn down the heat and put the lid on. If it is still dry, add a touch of water or butter.

- Chop mushrooms into small pieces and add after 3-5 minutes. Stir every couple of minutes. Salt and pepper to taste once they begin to soften. Keep lid on as needed to hold in moisture.

- Chop the rest of celery and all the carrots into bite size pieces and add. Cook 5-7 minutes covered, stirring 2-3 times.

- Take the lid off, turn up heat and add the sherry. Stir and boil it off, 3-4 minutes. Scrape up any browned bits. Add broth and bring soup to a boil. Adjust heat to maintain a gentle boil.

- As the soup heats, shred the chicken. Add it to the pot along with the rice, mustard, and tarragon.

THE ROUX/BÉCHAMEL

- Melt the butter in a 1½ quart saucepan. Add flour and cook gently 3-5 minutes, stirring every 15 -30 seconds with a whisk. Adjust heat so flour doesn't brown or burn, but gets a golden hue.

- Add the first 2 cups milk one at a time, stirring constantly. Add the second cup when the sauce starts to thicken. Stir constantly. Add remaining 2 cups once the sauce is thick again. Keep an eye on it and stir every 15-30 seconds. Bring it to a gentle boil and stir constantly for about a minute as it froths madly.

- Hopefully the soup is boiling by now and you can add the béchamel. Add a little water to the empty pan if a bunch of the sauce stuck and use a rubber spatula to loosen and re-cream it— then add it to the soup.

- Adjust seasonings and let simmer 5-15 minutes.

SHORTCUT OPTION

- Add the sherry once the onions and celery are soft. Cook about half of it off then add the broth, the rest of the celery, the mushrooms, and carrots. Gently boil and let all soften. Proceed with shredding the chicken. You'll need to check seasonings this way and may need to salt and pepper.

HYDRATING DRY MUSHROOMS

- Remove any peppercorns or other spices from the mushrooms. Put mushrooms in a small saucepan and barely cover with water. Bring to a gentle boil, turn off, and cover. Let the pan sit for about 20 minutes, pushing the softening mushrooms into the water several times.

- Drain mushrooms well, removing any grit, and save the water for stock. Proceed as with raw mushrooms, chopping and sautéing, etc.

Onion Soup

*S*tockton has long been a big onion growing area. Legend has it that the University of the Pacific campus was built on an onion field donated to the college (formerly located near San Jose) by an alumnus. Stockton Reds and Torpedo onions as well as other varieties start being harvested in April and are available fresh in the farmers' markets through June. They are still available most of the summer. I never buy onions in the grocery store when I can get them fresh from the farmer. They cook up so much more quickly and have an exquisite delicate flavor and texture. This is one of my favorite late spring — early summer soups.

INGREDIENTS

Makes 5 quarts, serves 12+

5 T butter/olive oil mix

5 lbs large onions, sliced

2 t sea salt

1 t pepper

2 t sugar

2 cloves garlic, minced

6 T flour

3+ quarts heated vegetable or beef stock

1 c dry white wine, room temp

OR ½ c Madeira or sherry

OR 1 quart beer (reduce stock by 3 cups)

½ t dried thyme or 1½ t fresh or 1 sprig thyme

2 sprigs parsley

1 bay leaf

salt and pepper to taste

12 slices crusty French bread

4½ ounces Swiss cheese, sliced 1/16th inch thick

1½ ounces Asiago cheese, grated (about ¾ cup)

INGREDIENT OPTIONS

• Add 2-4 cups well-cooked seasoned white beans.

• Add 1-2 lbs cooked shredded beef.

• Any flavor cheese will work on the croutons - blue, cheddar, brie, Boursin (don't bake), muenster.

• Using homemade broth adds so much to this if that is an option.

preparation on next page . . .

PREPARATION

- Sauté onions in butter in Dutch oven over medium to medium-low heat until tender and golden yellow, about 30-40 minutes. Stir often and use the lid if things get dry.

- Once they start to soften (15-20 minutes), stir in sugar, salt, and pepper.

- Sprinkle flour over onions. Cook a few minutes more, browning the flour well. Add stock and wine and bring to boil.

- Add thyme and bay leaf. Tie the parsley and thyme sprigs together with kitchen twine for easy removal.

- Reduce heat, cover, and simmer gently for 20-40 minutes. Add salt and pepper to taste.

- Toast bread in a 325 oven on a parchment lined tray for 12-15 minutes. Turn after 7 minutes and spread the top side with a little olive oil or butter, if desired.

- The toasts can also be rubbed with a large cut garlic clove.

CROUTON OPTION A

- When soup is almost ready, turn the oven to 475. Sprinkle/spread most of the cheeses onto the croutons and put them back in the oven to melt the cheese.

- Serve the soup, sprinkling the remaining cheese into each bowl. Put the crouton on top and push it in a bit. Let soup rest a couple of minutes to let the bread soften.

CROUTON OPTION B

- When soup is almost ready, turn the oven to 450. Put soup into oven- proof bowls and put a crouton in each one. Sprinkle with cheese.

- Place bowls on cookie sheet and bake for 8-10 until cheese is bubbly and golden. Broil if needed, but keep your eye on it!

Lunch at the "Low-Table Café" in front of "El Capitan", Yosemite National Park, California

Brown Tepary Bean or Lentil Soup

This was my "go to" lentil soup recipe, which then became my standard for green lentils. I'm happy to find that it transitions flawlessly to being a Tepary bean soup. The teparies lend a lovely amber tone to the dish.

INGREDIENTS

Makes 5-6 quarts

THE TEPARY BEANS

bouquet garni; fresh thyme, oregano, sage, bay, parsley (some or all of the above)

2 cloves garlic

1 lb lentils or Tepary beans (see note about varieties and cooking modifications)

8 c water (plus more later)

¾ c einkorn farro or brown rice, optional

2 more cups water if adding rice

2 t sea salt

THE SAUTÉ

2+ T olive oil

16 oz onion or 3 large leeks

6 cloves garlic minced (about 1½ T)

1 cup very small-dice celery

2-4 red, yellow or green peppers, optional

2-4+ jalapeños, minced, optional

8 oz very small-diced (2 cups) or grated carrots

½+ t sea salt, ¼ t fresh ground pepper

THE SOUP

½ t red pepper flakes

14 oz can or 1 lb fresh tomatoes, diced small

Salt and pepper to taste—1+ t salt per qt water, less if using salted broth

8 oz chard, spinach, escarole or savoy cabbage, thinly sliced, optional

1-4 cups small-chop or shredded, smoked ham hock/turkey leg/ham, optional

2-5 cups cooking bean water, broth or water

LENTIL VARIETIES

• I like to make the lentil version of this soup with less widely available lentil varieties. French, Green, Umbrian, and Beluga lentils are smaller and rounder, and don't disintegrate like regular lentils. Their outer "bite" and internal creaminess are a wonderful combination. If you can't get any of these lentils, regular ones work fine— just shorten the first cook time to 25 min.

GRAIN OPTIONS

• Adding einkorn farro (or brown rice) adds even more substance to the soup, especially for a vegetarian version. Another option is to cook the grain separately and serve it under the soup, or put a spoonful of it on top as Cajuns do with their Gumbos.

preparation on next page . . .

PREPARATION

COOK THE BEANS

- Tie together herbs at the stem end with kitchen string (to pull out the stems easily later).
- Combine herbs, garlic, beans, rice, water, and salt in a 6 quart pot. Bring to a boil and lower to maintain a very gentle boil for 45 minutes, or until beans are cooked.
- This can be made ahead, cooled and refrigerated.

MAKE THE SAUTÉ, THEN THE SOUP

- Start chopping the onions and other vegetables for the sauté. I like to chop things pretty small for this soup since the beans are little too, but it is personal preference.
- In a large sauté or the soup pot, heat olive oil on medium. Add the onions, stir and cook 3-5 minutes to soften. Salt and pepper, add garlic and cook 1-2 minutes more. Add celery and peppers; cook 4-6 minutes, stirring several times. Add the carrots.
- If things seem too dry, add a little more oil or about ¼ cup water/white wine, turn it down and put the lid on. Cook until carrots begin to soften. Turn off heat. Thinly slice greens.
- Combine sauté and cooked beans/rice. Add red pepper flakes, tomatoes, greens and meat if using. Also add 2-5 cups broth or water to achieve a stew like consistency. Gently simmer 30 - 45 minutes from this point, adding water/broth to your liking.
- Choose one of seasoning options below and add at the right time.

COOK'S NOTES

- There are several seasoning options. Read through and choose one before starting, so you add ingredients at the right time.
- If you want to use raw sausage, cook it in with the onions. You may need less oil. If the sausage is smoked, brown and add it in the last 15 minutes.
- The amount of liquid depends on the ingredients, the weather etc. Use as much as needed/desired. Any leftovers will thicken considerably.
- About using Tepary beans: Soak overnight (refrigerated) in 8 cups water, and extend first cook time as needed.

SEASONING OPTIONS - CHOOSE ONE:

■ *Marianne's Agrodolce*
- Add in for the last 30 min

¼-½ cup red wine

juice of 1 lemon

2 T red wine vinegar

1½ T brown sugar

fresh parsley/scallions at serving

1-2 T chevre per bowl at serving

■ *Bistro Jeanty's*
- Add in final 15 min

1 t cumin

1 t grated lemon peel

2 T fresh cilantro at serving

■ *Wolfgang Puck's*
- Add in just before serving

parsley, basil or chives at serving

parmesan at serving

■ *Lemon Herb*

1 t cumin; add to the sauté
- Add in final 15 minutes of cooking

3-4 T lemon juice
- Add at serving

4 T fresh parsley

3 T mint

top with yogurt

Chilled Zucchini Soup

A cold soup can be absolutely perfect on a hot summer evening. For this I used a 6-lb thigh-sized Romanesco zucchini that went unnoticed in my garden while I was out of town. After cutting out the pithy, seedy, center, the flesh made a wonderful soup - great for dinner and lunch the next day, too!

PREP EQUIPMENT NOTES

- This is a quick prep, but needs 1+ hour to chill.
- A food processor is needed.

INGREDIENTS

Makes 8 cups, 4-6 servings

3 lbs zucchini

½ t salt

1 T unsalted butter

4-6 oz white or yellow onion, small chop

1½ t fresh tarragon

¾ t salt

⅜ t white pepper

4-5 ounces cream cheese

¼-⅓ cup dry white wine

2-3 oz thawed peas or spinach for color

1-1⅓ cups cooking water

AT SERVING
(DON'T OMIT THE FIRST TWO)

1 T chopped fresh parsley (chives OK)

1 t finely grated lemon zest

2 t white truffle oil, optional

PREPARATION

- Put zucchini and salt in a sauté pan with not quite enough water to cover. Bring to a boil. Lower heat and simmer 2-3 minutes. Drain and set aside.
- Heat butter in the sauté pan, add the onions and sauté them. After 3 minutes, add the tarragon, salt, and white pepper. Cook another 2-3 minutes until onions are soft and translucent.
- In a food processor or blender, purée the zucchini and onions. Add cream cheese, wine, spinach/peas. Do batches if needed. Purée until the soup is velvety, 2-3 minutes.
- NOTE: This totally filled my blender. I waited and added 1 c broth once it was in a bigger container. No broth needed to purée it! Add broth as needed and test seasonings.
- Chill the soup thoroughly. You can freeze 1 hour in wide container.
- Chop the herbs and zest the lemon.
- Serve the soup garnished with a drizzle of truffle oil, the lemon zest, and parsley.

Corn Tomatillo Soup

INGREDIENTS

Makes 5-6 quarts

8 Anaheim chilies, roasted; about 1½ lbs raw

24 oz cooked corn; frozen or about 8 ears

10 oz frozen peas, thawed

20 oz onion, chopped (about 6 cups)

4 garlic cloves, diced

2 jalapeños, chopped, or more to taste

2-4 T butter

2 lbs tomatillos, husked and quartered

8-10 cups vegetable or chicken broth

4-6 T cilantro, chopped

4 oz spinach, chopped

1-3 t sugar, optional

1-1½ lb poached, seasoned shredded chicken, optional

Sea salt, fresh-ground pepper, and Mexican spice

Garnish options: tortilla chips, sour cream, chopped cilantro

PREPARATION

- Husk and quarter tomatillos. Soak them in water for a minute to make husking easy.

- Sauté onion, garlic, and jalapeño in butter.

- Add tomatillos and 2 cups of the broth to the onion sauté once they have softened. Season to taste.

- Chop cilantro and spinach while tomatillos cook to soft, about 10 minutes.

- Add corn, chiles, and 4 cups broth once tomatillos are soft.

- If puréeing in blender or food processor, begin in batches, adding peas, cilantro, and spinach as you go.

- If using immersion blender, add in peas, cilantro, spinach, and 2-4 cups more broth, and puree to desired consistency.

- Stir in shredded chicken, if using. Season to taste.

- Reheat as needed, garnish if desired, and serve.

TO ROAST CHILES

- Chiles can be roasted over an open flame, under a broiler, or on a bbq grill at 450-500 degrees.

- Check the chiles every 2 minutes and turn them with tongs as they blacken. They should take 10 minutes, but may take as long as 20 depending on the heat.

- Put the blackened chiles, as they are done, into a paper bag that is inside a plastic bag.

- Let cool and then peel. Be careful not to rub your face or you may get burned if chiles are hot.

- Roasted chiles will keep several days covered in the refrigerator.

COOK'S NOTES

- Anaheim chiles have a little heat, which is key to the soup's flavor. If using an all-sweet variety, replace 2 or 3 of them with poblanos. In any case, don't use bell peppers.

- If adding chicken, I purée the soup roughly. If not adding chicken and serving as a first course, try puréeing it very smoothly.

Barley Mushroom Soup

*This is comfort food as good as it gets!
Added meat or beans are strictly optional.
I love it with the winter squash and greens,
if I have them on hand.*

INGREDIENTS

Makes 4-5 quarts

• Barley and the optional garbanzos can be made
ahead and refrigerated.

1¼ cup barley, about ½ lb.

16 oz mushrooms

2 oz dried Porcini or other mushrooms
or 10 oz fresh mushrooms

2+ T flavorful olive oil

sea salt and red or freshly ground black pepper

8 oz onion, chopped

8 oz leek (2 med/lg) or may substitute onion

6 oz celery (3 lg stalks)

6 oz carrots; omit if using winter squash

1 cup sherry

8 cups good broth; store bought low sodium is
fine; more may be needed the next day

½ t dry mustard

½-1 t tarragon

OPTIONAL INGREDIENTS

1 lb leftover roast beef, chicken,
or turkey

1½-3 cups pre-cooked garbanzo
beans or corn

¾ - 1 lb peeled, cubed, cooked
winter squash

8-12 oz small-chopped greens

PREPARATION

• Cook barley and, if using, hydrate dry mushrooms; see below for
instructions.

• If using roast beef, small chop and sauté (in the soup pot) in two
batches with a little olive oil to get it crispy. Remove and set aside.
Don't rinse the pot.

• Small chop the onions and begin to sauté them on medium to
medium-high heat in some of the olive oil. If using, quarter the
white part of the leek lengthwise and then thinly chop it crosswise.
If you see any sand or dirt, rinse and drain the cut leeks well. Add to
the sauté. Chop ⅓ of the celery into tiny pieces and add after things
just start to soften. Season with a bit of salt and pepper. Add olive
oil as needed.

• If things get dry, turn down the heat, add a touch of water or wine
and put the lid on.

continued on next page . . .

COOK'S NOTES

TO HYDRATE DRY MUSHROOMS

- Remove any peppercorns or other spices from the mushrooms. Put mushrooms in a small saucepan and barely cover with water. Bring to a gentle boil, turn off, and cover. Let the pan sit for about 20 minutes, pushing the softening mushrooms into the water several times.

- Drain mushrooms well (avoid any grit), and save the water for stock. Proceed as with raw mushrooms, chopping and sautéing, etc.

TO MAKE BARLEY

- In a 2 quart saucepan, combine 1¼ cups (half the 1 lb bag) with 2¾ cups water and ½ t salt. Cover and bring to a boil. Simmer 45 minutes.

TO PEEL WINTER SQUASH

- Some people find these easier to peel by first microwaving them, whole or halved, 3-5 minutes, and letting them rest 30 minutes.

- A sharp potato peeler is favored over a knife by some. But a dull peeler doesn't help at all!

- Chop mushrooms into small pieces and add once the sauté has started to soften, even crisp. Turn up the heat if the mushrooms start to "make water." Stir every couple of minutes. Salt and pepper to taste once they begin to soften. Cook until the water is gone and things are again a bit crisped.

- Add the sherry. Stir and boil it off, 3-4 minutes. Scrape up any browned bits.

- Chop the rest of celery and the carrots/winter squash (peel it first) into small bite size pieces.

- Add broth, celery, carrots/squash, cover and bring soup to a boil. Adjust heat to achieve a gentle but steady boil. Check the carrots and winter squash after 6-8 minutes, and when they are almost soft enough, add the barley and corn/garbanzos. Lower to heat bring soup to a simmer for 10 minutes.

- Next, add meat and greens, if using, along with the mustard and tarragon. Taste and adjust seasonings as needed (probably will need salt and pepper unless broth was quite seasoned).

- Simmer 5-15 minutes. Soup can be eaten now or cooled, refrigerated, and enjoyed later.

- Serve with a crisp salad and crusty bread.

- 2-3 cups water may need to be added the next day.

- Freeze after 3 days.

Marianne in Hudson, New York, 2015

Gazpacho

Another cold soup perfect for a summer evening. Proportions of the vegetables are just guidelines. Freshness and peak of flavor are the important things.

INGREDIENTS

Makes 3 quarts

4 lbs tomatoes

5 cloves garlic

2 t salt

4 oz STALE French bread

1¼ lbs cucumber

1½ lbs red peppers - OK to have a green one in the mix

¼ c diced onions, optional

1 jalapeño, optional

5 T olive oil

4 T sherry vinegar, may sub red wine vinegar

1+ t salt, ¼+ t black pepper

¼+ t cayenne pepper

GARNISH OPTIONS

½ lb small cooked shrimp

Chives, scallions, or parsley

PREPARATION

- Core and chop tomatoes, put into bowl, and lightly salt (1 t). I do not seed them, but you can, if you prefer. Save any juices and add back to the bowl.

- Chop peppers, including jalapeño if using (core, seed). Chop cukes (peel and seed). Chop onion.

- Mash garlic with salt.

- Tear bread into the bowl of a food processor. Add the garlic and any juices from the chopped tomatoes. Pulse to mash the bread. Add a tomato or two for moisture and keep pulsing until it is all mushed.

- Add about ¼ of each (tomato, cucumber, pepper, onion) to processor and process until smooth. Pour out about ¾ of the mixture into a 4-6 quart bowl or pot.

- Add another ¼ of each, as well as ⅓ of the olive oil. Process and add to bowl. Repeat twice.

- Stir the bowl with a large slotted spoon and if there are any non-puréed pieces, put them back in the processor.

- Add the vinegar with the last group.

- Add about 1 cup water to wash out the processor and add that to the bowl.

- Season to taste with salt and pepper.

- Chill soup at least 2 hours and chill the bowls 30+ minutes.

Marianne working at Café La Fraise, Hanover, New Hampshire, 1983

White Gazpacho

I had a bumper crop of Armenian cucumbers (that's 9 lbs of them!), so this soup was a no-brainer. It is delicious and keeps well for 4-6 days. There are lots of garnish options — find your favorite!

INGREDIENTS *Makes 10 cups*

4 lbs English, Persian, or Armenian cucumbers

2 oz baguette

½ cup raw almonds

3 cloves garlic, or more to taste

1-2 serrano or jalapeño peppers

1 small shallot or 2 T chopped red onion

1½ cups green grapes, optional

1 stem fresh basil—pull out before blending

3 short mint stems—pull out before blending

2 cups ice water, more as needed to thin

6 T sherry vinegar

1 c Arbequina olive oil

2 t sea salt and ⅔ pepper, or to taste

½-⅔ cup mild flavored white wine (or water)

SERVING GARNISH OPTIONS

Need 1-2 cups total

lump crab, razor clam ezcabeche, sliced grapes, serrano ham, fresh cilantro leaf, marcona almonds, borage flowers

ALMOND CRUNCH INGREDIENTS

3 oz whole-grain bread

½ cup raw or marcona almonds

SOUP PREP

• Blanch the garlic by putting it in a ⅓ cup measure and covering it with boiling water. Let sit 2 minutes and strain off the hot water. Repeat 5 times to remove the "raw" flavor.

• Cut cukes in half crosswise if longer than 8". Peel and then quarter top to bottom. Cut out any seed line. Use to make a cooling pitcher of cucumber water and enjoy!

• Small-chop the cucumbers and put in a container with a lid that seals well. Chop and add the garlic, onions, grapes if using, serranos, bread crumbs, basil and mint sprigs, olive oil, vinegar, and water. Mix well. Let sit overnight.

• Dice the bread crumbs and toast with the almonds in the oven or on the stove to brown with 1 T olive oil, sea salt and freshly ground pepper.

• In the morning, pull out herb sprigs and stir in the breadcrumbs and almonds and let rest 30-45 minutes more.

• Purée the mixture in batches adding grapes, if using, and thinning with wine as needed.

• Purée as little or as much as desired. Soup can be put through a sieve if desired to make it extra velvety (You will lose about 2 cups of the yield).

• Let the soup sit refrigerated all day, then season to taste.

ALMOND CRUNCH PREP

• Cut 3 oz of day-old whole-grain bread into pieces and pulse with ½ cup almonds in a food processor to a small or medium-sized crumb. Toast to golden and crispy, stirring every 30 seconds, for 4-8 minutes in a sauté pan in 2+ T olive oil.

Marianne Hard at Play

◀ Biking near Taos, New Mexico

▼ Windsurfing with Dave at the Delta

▼ Standup paddle boarding in Lake Tahoe, California

▶ Hiking near Half Moon Bay, California

▶ Skiing with Dave at Alpine Meadows, California

Sensational Salads

Rustic Borlotti Bean Salad

*T*his recipe is a perfect example of a few top quality ingredients making all the difference. *Borlottis are huge, tan beans, beautifully speckled with red. They are sometimes referred to as "cranberry beans". Borlottis have a creamy texture and a sweetish flavor, and play oh-so-well off the simple minced vegetables and parsley.*

INGREDIENTS

Makes about 6 cups

1 lb heirloom borlotti beans

⅓ c roasted garlic olive oil

1 bay leaf

2-3 cloves garlic

2 T red or sherry wine vinegar

1 t grey or pink sea salt, to taste

½ t fresh ground black pepper, or to taste

2 T mild red pepper flakes

¾ c minced red or white onion

1 cup minced bell pepper (red, yellow, or green)

½-1 c minced celery

½ c minced parsley - can use some basil or cilantro

PREPARATION

• Beans can be cooked ahead, but this salad is extra special if the oil and vinegar are poured on the beans while they are still warm.

• Soak beans overnight or do the quick soak method (bring to a boil for one or two minutes, then turn off heat and let rest 1 hour).

• Cook following package directions. Add a bay leaf and 2 or 3 cloves garlic if available.

• Mince vegetables and herbs as beans cook.

• Once beans are cooked, add salt and let sit uncovered in the broth 10-20 minutes.

• After the rest, drain the beans (save broth for stock) and add in the oil and vinegar. Let cool to warm and add the rest of the ingredients.

• Enjoy at room temperature or cold.

• Add extra vinegar as needed but sparingly if the salad needs a little perking up.

COOK'S NOTES

• If desired, add small chunks of garden fresh tomatoes or lightly steamed chopped green beans or whatever delicious fresh vegetable you happen to have on hand. Add more oil, vinegar and seasoning as needed for the extra vegetables.

• This mix also works well with garbanzo beans.

Blue Christmas Lima Salad

This is truly a "sensational" and simple salad that can be enjoyed all year long, especially if you grow mint, or find friends who do. Many people are not familiar with this gorgeous white and dark-red speckled variety of Limas. Their beautiful patterns are maintained during cooking. They still have that lima meaty texture, but with a rich chestnut-like flavor — hence the name "Christmas".

INGREDIENTS

Serves 10-12, about 6 cups

1 lb Christmas lima beans

1 t sea salt or to taste

⅓ cup Blood Orange Olive Oil or similar flavorful olive oil

2 T sherry wine vinegar - or other wine vinegar

½ t sea salt and ¼ t ground black pepper, or to taste

½ cup finely chopped fresh mint

¾ cup roasted hazelnuts, chopped

3 oz crumbled blue cheese

PREPARATION

• Soak beans overnight and cook according to package directions. Christmas limas take 75-90 minutes to cook, so be patient.

• Salt once they are done. Cool in liquid.

• Beans can be cooked, cooled and stored covered in the refrigerator for up to 3 days. Or the salad can be assembled as soon as the beans cool to warm.

• Mix oil, vinegar, salt and pepper and pour over warm or cool drained beans.

• Chop mint, nuts and crumble blue cheese by scraping the block gently with a fork.

• Combine all the ingredients and enjoy with lunch, dinner, or on a party buffet.

COOK'S NOTES

• More vinegar may be needed after a day or so, if the salad loses its perk. Add 1 teaspoon at a time *(you can't take away too much)*. You can also add a little more oil to revive the wonderful orange flavor.

• While this recipe is complete as it is, you can also consider it as a base and build on it with what you have on hand or what you think will go well from a color, flavor, or texture standpoint. Plan to make more vinaigrette and add extra mint if you add a lot more "stuff" to the salad.

Garbanzo (Chick Pea) Salad

In the spring and early summer, fresh garbanzos can be found in farmers' markets and at Indian grocery stores. They take time to shuck but their beautiful green color and super fresh taste are wonderful. No need to soak these, just boil gently for 20-30 minutes.

This salad is simple and delicious. The dressing is strong and melds wonderfully with the onions and garbanzos.

Improvise and add other raw small-chopped vegetables - carrots, broccoli, or even some romaine lettuce. This dish is best if flavors have a chance to meld overnight, so plan ahead.

INGREDIENTS

Makes about 3 cups, serves 4-8

THE SALAD

1¼ cup dried garbanzos, cooked OR two 15 oz cans garbanzos

½ cup minced onion

½ cup chopped parsley, at serving

THE DRESSING

• *This makes double what you actually need*

2 garlic cloves

2 oz anchovy fillets, drained

1 hard-boiled egg, peeled and coarsely chopped

¼ c sherry wine vinegar

2 T Dijon mustard

2 T lemon juice

1 t dried thyme or 1 T fresh

2 bay leaves well chopped

1 cup minced parsley

PREPARATION

• Mix chick peas and onion in a bowl.

• Combine dressing ingredients in a small food processor or blender. Pour about half of the dressing over the chick peas. Cover and refrigerate overnight.

• Stir in parsley at serving.

Marinne in San Miguel de Allende, Mexico, 2010

Farro, Red Bean & Feta Salad

This recipe came from a magazine ad and originally used a box of seasoned bulgur as a base. I first remember having it after a day of mountain biking in Idaho when I was traveling across America. I made it with bulgur until I was making a large batch for a wedding. When I went to buy bulgur, the store was out of stock. . . I saw couscous and thought I'd give it a try and it was a huge hit. Feel free to substitute brown rice, couscous or bulgur for the farro.

COOK'S NOTES

- Soak and cook dry beans or use two 15 oz cans. If you soak the farro beforehand, that will reduce the cooking time by about 30%.

- Both the beans and grains can be prepared ahead.

- The salad is wonderful warm, cool, or at room temperature. I take a portion out of the refrigerator and let it warm for 15 minutes or so before eating.

- If the salad loses its perk, sprinkle on a little red wine vinegar, or add a squeeze of fresh lemon or orange juice.

SALAD INGREDIENTS

Makes 8+ cups

3 cups cooked red beans; ½ lb. (approx. 1 ⅓ cup) raw

1½ cups farro, uncooked

¾ t salt

3 cups water

½ cup toasted walnuts

½ + cup finely chopped cilantro

⅓ cup very finely chopped red onion

4-6 oz crumbled feta cheese

6-12 oz top quality canned or poached tuna, optional

VINAIGRETTE INGREDIENTS

1 ½ t fresh crushed garlic, about 2 cloves

3 T flavorful extra virgin olive oil (see below for a delicious Blood Orange Option!)

2 T red wine vinegar, or to taste

½ t sea salt and ¼ t pepper, or more to taste

PREPARATION

- Soak the beans in a quart of water overnight in a cool place.

- Simmer beans with a bay leaf until cooked.

- Combine farro, water and salt in a 1.5 quart saucepan with a lid. Bring to a boil and simmer covered, about an hour. Let sit until ready to use. Drain off any extra liquid and save for soup.

- Toast and chop the walnuts.

- Chop the cilantro, onion & garlic (for vinaigrette).

- Rinse the tuna if using, crumble the feta.

- Mix ingredients for the vinaigrette.

- Combine everything.

- Taste and adjust seasonings.

Warm Green Lentil Salad

There is something so earthy and comforting about lentils. They are a great foil for the spicy greens and the salty feta cheese. Enjoy them warm in this classic French salad for lunch, as a hearty snack or as a dinner side dish.

INGREDIENTS

Makes 4-6 cups

THE LENTILS

1 cup green or beluga lentils

5 cups water

¾ t sea salt

1 medium onion (4-8 oz)

1 large or 2 small carrots

1 sprig thyme

1 bay leaf

12 sprigs parsley, divided

THE VINAIGRETTE

1 T red wine or sherry vinegar

1½ t Dijon mustard

2½ T olive oil

Sea salt and fresh ground pepper

1 or 2 finely chopped scallions or shallots

OTHER SALAD INGREDIENTS

4 oz arugula or escarole

½ head radicchio

1 endive or 2 oz escarole

5 oz crumbled feta

PREPARATION

• Fill a 2 quart pot with 5 cups water and the lentils.

• Halve the onion, leaving a piece of the root end on each side to hold it together and remove the peel. Scrub and cut the carrots into 4 or 5 chunks.

• Add these, the bay, thyme and 2 sprigs parsley to the pot. Let it simmer gently 25-40 minutes until lentils are tender.

• Remove herbs and vegetables from lentil mix once it cools a bit.

• While the lentils cook, mix the vinaigrette ingredients. Steal a few tablespoons of the thickening lentil broth and whisk that in.

• Chop the remaining parsley, chiffonade (fine long slices) the greens, and crumble the feta.

• Drain the warm lentils, saving some broth to add back if needed.

• Gently combine the greens, cheese, warm lentils and vinaigrette. Add the extra liquid if needed.

• Taste and adjust seasonings each time you serve the salad.

COOK'S NOTES

• Assertive greens of any type will work - mix and match endive, arugula, escarole, frisse, or radicchio as available.

• This salad is best warm or at room temperature. Give it time to lose the chill if it has been refrigerated.

• For a quick snack, warm a serving in the microwave for 15-20 seconds.

• Try substituting lemon juice or white wine vinegar for the red wine vinegar.

• Serve topped with quartered hard-boiled eggs.

• Try adding steamed green beans.

• Thinly sliced and sautéed red onion also makes a nice addition. While it cooks, sprinkle the onion with red wine vinegar to help hold the color.

Mississippi "Caviar"

Sort of salad, sort of dip on chips, this is a wonderful way to eat your beans, especially when they are fresh in our farmers' markets (late summer). I made this batch using beans that I grew and dried. Since there were no local peppers in the markets yet, I substituted a jar of Sondra's Salsa. Sondra is another Stocktonian who makes this fantastic salsa - available in mild and spicy. It is really good!

INGREDIENTS

2 T olive oil

2 t red wine vinegar

½ t dried thyme - 1½ t fresh

sea salt and and fresh ground pepper

1 clove minced garlic

2 cups cooked black eyed peas or one 18 oz can, rinsed and drained

¼ minced red onion or scallion (green and white)

⅔ cup minced red, yellow, or green sweet peppers

¼ cup chopped parsley

¼ cup minced celery, optional

1-4 minced jalapenos, to taste

PREPARATION

• Mix first four ingredients in a small cup and set aside.

• Put the black-eyed peas in a mixing bowl. Save their cooking broth for soup if you soaked and cooked them. Otherwise drain and rinse well. Gently mash if desired (for dip version).

• Mince onions and add to vinaigrette.

• Mince peppers, celery, parsley and jalapeno (do last) and mix with the black eyed peas.

• Wash hands thoroughly after handling the jalapenos to avoid a burning sensation on your fingertips - and any place else you touch. It's the flesh and white pith that are the worst culprits.

• Pour vinaigrette over. Taste - it should be quite strong.

• Let salad stand several hours. Taste again and add seasonings as needed.

• If using as a dip, gently mash the mixture if desired. Serve with corn chips.

COOKS NOTES

• If using dry beans, soak and cook up to three days ahead.

• Salad needs time to meld for best flavor, so try to make the night before or earlier in the day.

• This recipe offers lots of room for modification; Use black beans, use prepared salsa instead of the sweet peppers, add corn; blend the beans a bit to make it smooth for dipping. Whatever your pleasure, just enjoy more beans!

Warm White Bean Salad

This salad is a delicious accompaniment to grilled or roasted meats or a light meal with some of the add-ins listed below. In this photo, I added pasta to the salad. Eat it warm or cold, but most find that beans taste richest if not ice cold. Runner Cannellini beans are a bigger, flatter, beautiful, white, heirloom variety of cannellinis, with a luscious flavor and texture. Try them and you will be hooked!

INGREDIENTS

Makes about 3 cups - double for a crowd

½ lb (about 1⅓ cup) Runner Cannellini, Mayocoba or White Romano Beans

2 bay leaves

3 cloves garlic

THE HERB VINAIGRETTE

3 T flavorful olive oil

3 T lemon juice or wine vinegar

1 clove garlic, mashed

½ t sea salt

⅛ t fresh ground pepper, to taste

pinch of cayenne or other spicy red pepper

2-8 T fresh herbs, minced; I like a 2 T thyme, sage, oregano mix or a 6 T parsley basil mix

PREPARATION

• Soak dry beans overnight in a cool place in 3+ cups water.

• Cook beans in a 1.5 quart pot with bay leaves, garlic and water to cover by 2". Add more water, if needed. Partly cover the pan and gently boil until soft to the bite, 35-90 minutes depending on the bean. Skim off foam with a slotted spoon.

• Make the vinaigrette and chop the herbs.

• When the beans are to your taste, scoop them into a bowl and toss with the vinaigrette and herbs.

• Add other ingredients as desired. This can be done when beans are warm or cool.

OPTIONAL ADD-IN INGREDIENTS

• If you add 3+ cups more items, make another batch of vinaigrette and add to taste.

1-2 c cooked chunky pasta or cooked waxy potatoes

1 can good quality solid tuna or 1-2 cups cooked shrimp

1-4 c cooked green beans

1-5 c diced flavorful tomatoes

½ c coarse chopped oil-cured black olives

1 c shaved goat cheese, feta or ricotta salata

Warm White Bean, Chestnut, and Mushroom Salad

At a wine and food pairing that I cooked for, one of the guests said he could bring me chestnuts from his Dad's ranch. I wasted no time developing a recipe featuring chestnuts, for a luncheon I was preparing to cater. This dish incorporates chestnuts, wild mushrooms, fennel, fresh spinach, and Runner Cannelini or other white beans.

INGREDIENTS

Makes about 8 cups (2½ lbs), 8-12 servings

1 ⅓ cup dry white beans

1 small onion

1 small carrot

1 bay leaf

5 cloves garlic minced

½ lb chestnuts, peeled, roasted & coarsely chopped (see roasting instructions on following page)

1 large fennel bulb (10-12 oz trimmed)

1 T olive oil

½ white or yellow onion, diced (about 3 oz)

½ lb chanterelle or yellow foot mushrooms - may substutute white or cremini

splash or 3 of Pernod (herb and licorice liqueur)

juice of ½ Meyer lemon juice

salt and pepper

4 oz baby spinach or baby frisee

COOK'S NOTES

• As with many dishes, this tastes best if made ahead and gently reheated when serving. Wait to add the greens until just before serving.

• Beans can be soaked and cooked ahead. Chestnuts can be roasted & peeled ahead too.

PREPARATION

• Soak beans overnight. Simmer with listed vegetables covered in plenty of water until tender.

• Roast chestnuts; link and details on following page.

• Chop the fennel, onions, garlic and chestnuts.

• In a large skillet, sauté fennel, onion & garlic, but not to color.

• If your pan is not large enough, season to taste and remove the fennel before proceeding.

• Add the mushrooms and salt lightly. When they start to sweat, add the chestnuts. Stir gently and sauté until mushrooms are limp and chestnut pieces are soft. Add fennel back in if you removed it. Add Pernod and lemon juice and cook off. Season as needed.

• Fold together the sauté and beans.

• Dish can be made ahead to this point.

• Cool and refrigerate, covered, up to 2 days. Gently reheat and proceed.

• Fold in the greens and taste and adjust seasonings as needed. Serve warm.

Roasting Chestnuts

*C*hestnuts have a delicious, rustic, clean and earthy flavor. They are also gluten-free, low-fat, and a good source of protein, fiber, vitamins, and minerals. When chestnuts start appearing at farmers' markets, buy a batch and enjoy their sweet, nutty flavor, and health benefits.

COOK'S NOTES

- **IMPORTANT**: The chestnut roasting process described here gets the shell off, but you may want to sauté or roast them more, to your preference or for a particular recipe.

- 2 lbs raw nuts yields about 1 lb (2-2.5 cups) roasted peeled meats.

- They expand as you cook them more and really develop a nice, rich flavor.

- Chestnuts can be roasted and peeled up to 3 days ahead. Store refrigerated in a covered container.

- Buy 20-30% more chestnuts than you need because some won't score or peel properly, and you will want to snack on a few.

PREPARATION

- Rinse chestnuts and soak in water 10-15 minutes.

- Score each nut on the rounded side with an x that cuts through the shell and the skin, but not the meat.

- Chestnuts are traditionally roasted over open coals or a gas burner. They can also be roasted in the oven or on a BBQ grill.

- On the BBQ; preheat the grill to 400 and leave one burner off. Put the chestnuts over the off burner with all the x's up. Flip them using tongs every 5 minutes. They should be done in 20 minutes.

- In the oven: Preheat the oven to 425. Set the chestnuts on a tray or in a pan with the x up. Roast 20-30 minutes.

- The chestnuts are done when the cut shell and skin peel away to expose the flesh.

- Pile the hot chestnuts in a less than new kitchen towel and give it a couple of squeezes. The nuts should crackle. The towel will get hot but will hold moisture, in which helps release the skin.

- Peel them as soon as they are cool enough to touch. Don't let them cool completely before peeling.

- If the skins stick, dampen the towel and put the mass in the microwave for a minute or so or into a toaster oven at 300 to create a little steam.

Beet Apple Chevre Salad

This rosy salad has crisp and crunch, sweet and tangy and a whole host of bright colors to delight the eye. Enjoy at home and share at buffet parties. This is a display salad with endless options. Let your creativity go wild both in how you chop the apples and beets and how you plate or platter it.

SALAD INGREDIENTS

Serves 16+ on a buffet or 8 beet lovers

1½ lbs. pink beets

1¼ lbs. red beets

10 oz apple (about 2 medium)

3 oz walnuts

5 green onions;
   need ⅓ cup chopped

4 oz chevre cheese

VINAIGRETTE

3 T minced shallots

1 T white wine vinegar

½ c white wine vinegar

2½ T flavorful extra virgin olive oil - lemon or orange would be great!

¾ t sea salt

⅓ t pepper

⅓ t sugar

COOK'S NOTES

- Make the beets and marinate them the day before or early that day.

- This could be served atop 6-16 oz baby spinach leaves.

- Add cooked and seasoned shredded chicken for a main course salad.

PREPARATION

- Cook, skin and slice beets.

- Mince shallots and marinate in white wine vinegar while the beets are cooking.

- Put together vinaigrette too. After 20 minutes add the shallots and any vinegar they were in.

- Pour the vinaigrette over the beets and marinate 2 hours - overnight.

- Toast walnuts on a pie plate at 300 for 8 minutes or stovetop in a dry skillet. Watch to not burn!

- Chop walnuts and scallions. Break up cheese with a fork.

- Cut apples into 6 wedges top to bottom and cut out the core. Thinly slice crosswise. 5-45 minutes before serving, pour the marinade off the beets and onto the apples.

- Arrange or pile the beets onto a platter, then spoon out and spread the marinated apples on top. Next the cheese, the nuts, and the green onions. Drizzle the remaining dressing over the top.

Barley or Farro Beet Salad

T his salad is always a crowd-pleaser because of its taste, variety of textures and the vibrant, eye-catching color of the beets. Some people mis-identify it as having pomegranate seeds in it because of the crunch and shape of the grain. You can also use the salad as a sort of topping on a green salad.

INGREDIENTS

2 c minced beets (4 medium, 1 lb raw, about ⅔ lb cooked)

3 T raspberry or other fruit-infused Balsamic vinegar

1 T Blood Orange Olive Oil

¼ t red pepper flakes, optional / to taste

½ lb barley or emmer farro

½ t sea salt

VINAIGRETTE

⅓ cup red onion or 3 green onions

1½ t crushed garlic, about 2 cloves

2 T blood orange olive oil, or similar

2 T good red wine vinegar

¼ t sea salt

¼ t black pepper

¼ t red pepper, more to taste

AT SERVING

½ cup small chop roasted hazelnuts or walnuts

4-6 oz crumbled feta or blue cheese

12 oz fresh spinach or arugula leaves or other sturdy greens

COOK'S NOTES

• Much of this recipe can be made ahead. The beets and farro can be cooked and the nuts toasted a couple of days ahead. The beets need to marinate at least 4 hours and up to a day before serving. The grain can be tossed in the vinaigrette 15 minutes -12 hours before serving.

• The beets will turn everything a glorious shade of purple when you add them. Add the greens in the last 2-45 minutes so they don't get too wilted. There should be just enough dressing to give things a slight sheen, not a drench.

TO COOK BEETS, BARLEY, AND FARRO

• Leave root and 1 inch stem on beets; scrub with a brush. Place in a medium saucepan; cover with water. Bring to a boil; cover, reduce heat, and simmer 35 minutes or until tender. Drain and rinse with cold water, and cool. Trim off roots, and rub off skins. Cut into 1/3" cubes.

• Combine farro, 2.25 cups water and salt in a 1.5 quart saucepan with a lid. For barley, use 2.75 cups water. Bring to a boil and simmer covered, about an hour. Let sit until ready to use. Drain off any extra liquid and save for soup.

Recipe preparation continues on next page . . .

. . . Barley or Farro Beet Salad continued

PREPARATION

- Cook & pickle the beets at least four hours ahead. Cook the grain. Drain off any extra liquid and save for soup. (directions below)

- Toast and chop the nuts.

- Mince the onion & garlic and combine the vinaigrette. Let sit 15+ minutes to "soften" the onion and garlic. Mix with the nuts and grain up to 12 hours before serving.

- Thinly slice the greens (or not) if using and crumble the cheese.

- Combine everything.

- Taste and adjust seasonings.

Spicy Sweet Beet Salad

If your beet greens look good, roll in a towel and store refrigerated in a plastic bag. Use within a couple of days as beet greens don't last too long. To cook, rinse well, chop off & discard stems & any yellowed leaf parts. Chop the greens, shake off excess water and toss in a sauté for 3-5 minutes to wilt them. Then season to taste with sea salt and black or red pepper. Drizzle with some good olive oil, and splash with a bit of one of Marianne's or similar vinegars for a simple, delicious experience.

INGREDIENTS

Serves 8 as a side, less for vegetable & grain lovers

1¼ lbs. whole raw beets

¼ c raspberry or other fruit-infused Balsamic vinegar

1 T Blood Orange Olive Oil, or similar (optional)

¼ teaspoon Sri Racha or other hot sauce, optional/to taste

PREPARATION

- Simmer whole beets covered, in water for 30-45 minutes until softening. Drain and cool in a colander. Slip off skins and break off root end. This can be done up to two days ahead.

- Chop as desired.

- Combine remaining ingredients and pour over the beets. Stir to be sure all beets get in the sauce. Marinate 4+ hours.

- If desired, marinate them in a single layer; on a rimmed tray or glass baking dish.

- Adjust the hot sauce to your personal preference.

COOK'S NOTES

- Enjoy these beets as is or use them as a base for a more substantial salad.

- Stir into cooked farro or barley (yes it will all turn a ruby red color).

- Add crumbled feta or blue cheese, toasted chopped walnuts or hazelnuts.

- Toss with spinach leaves.

- Add a little good extra virgin olive oil, salt and pepper to taste.

Beet & Blue Cheese Salad with Fennel & Green Beans

This salad makes for a gorgeous presentation on a buffet or as a composed salad. And the flavors tantalize the palate at least as well as they do the eye. The fennel is a wonderful component, but if you can't find fresh crispy fennel (it is not a hot summer vegetable and can become tough and woody), just leave it out.

INGREDIENTS

Makes 8 Servings

¾ lb green beans

¼ (4 oz) fennel bulb, optional

1 lb beets

2 T minced shallots

⅓ cup champagne or white wine vinegar (may use ½ champagne orange muscat)

½ cup toasted walnuts, optional (do if no beans)

1½ T olive oil

3 oz blue cheese, divided ⅔, ⅓

OR sub chevre or feta (use less salt if feta)

¼ t sugar, ½ t salt, ¼ t pepper, to taste

PREPARATION

• Cook beets & beans ahead and this is a quickly assembled salad.

• Cook beets using the method of your choice. See below.

• When beets are cool, slide skins off and chop as desired - cubes, shoe strings or rounds.

• Blanch green beans 3 minutes in boiling salted water that doesn't quite cover them. Transfer to an ice water bath to prevent further cooking or loss of color.

• Once cool, set in a colander to dry. Leave beans whole or cut into shorter pieces.

• Core and thinly slice the fennel. Put in ice water to crisp 15-30 minutes.

• Chop shallots finely, mix with 1 T of the vinegar and let sit 15-30 minutes.

• Toast and chop walnuts if using.

• Crumble cheese with a fork or chop with a knife.

• Combine oil, the rest of the vinegar, and ⅔ of the cheese. Season with salt, pepper, and ½ t sugar.

preparation continued next page . . .

Beet and Blue Cheese Salad continued . . .

- 30+ minutes before serving, stir the shallots and 3/4 of the vinaigrette into the beets. After 15 minutes, test seasonings and adjust as needed.

- At the moment of serving, mix the fennel and most of the green beans into the beets.

- Decorate the top of the salad with the rest of the beans, the cheese and the nuts. Drizzle remaining dressing on top of all.

BEET COOKING METHODS:

MOIST OVEN ROAST

- Preheat oven to 375-400.

- Halve beets and put in an oven safe pan that just holds them cut side down in one layer. To save on clean up, line the pan with parchment that comes up the sides. Pour in water to come up ¾" on the beets. Cover the pan with a lid or foil and bake an hour or so until softened. Poke gently with knife or skewer to check.

GENTLE BOIL

- Trim stems to ¼". Leave root end on and keep beets whole. Fit into a pan with tight fitting lid that just holds them in one layer. Fill with water to cover beets about ¾ of the way up. Bring to a gentle boil. Check to be sure the water doesn't boil off. Test after 25 minutes by poking gently with a knife or a skewer. Cook until softened. Let sit in water covered 10-15 minutes, then transfer to another container or just remove the lid to cool.

Shredded Zucchini Salad with Meyer Lemon Olive Oil Vinaigrette

INGREDIENTS

1 lb zucchini

½ head green garlic or
  2 cloves garlic, optional

2 T fresh dill or basil

3 T minced onion, optional

2 T Meyer Lemon Olive Oil

1 T white wine vinegar

½ t sea salt

⅛+ t fresh ground black pepper

HEALTH BENEFITS OF ZUCCHINI

- Zucchini often gets a bad rap as such a common vegetable, but at only 17 calories/100 grams, and offering 30% of your vitamin C for the day, it is well worth eating. It is also a good source of the important electrolyte, potassium.

PREPARATION

- Grate zucchini in a food processor. Press hard on the zucchini to get a coarser result.

- Mince the garlic, onion and herbs and combine with the remaining ingredients to make the vinaigrette. Let this sit about 20 minutes to "cook" the onion and garlic.

- Toss into shredded zucchini.

- Add additional vinegar sparingly at serving. If you add too much up front and keep it around for a few days, it will get a pickled, not fresh, flavor.

Southwest Black Bean and Rice Salad

This salad is fantastic! I make it using Massa organic brown rice and Black Valentine heirloom beans. The recipe makes a huge quantity and takes a while to put together, but it is worth the work because it is so good! I only make it for parties and then hope for lots of leftovers. You can certainly half or quarter it as needed.

INGREDIENTS

*Makes 18-22 cups,
14 large servings*

- 1-2 lbs seasoned, cooked shrimp or shredded pork shoulder
- 3 c cooked, seasoned black beans
  - 10-12 oz (1 ⅓ cups) dry, soaked and cooked or 2 ½-3 cans, well rinsed
- 3-5 ears corn, to make 3 cups or 1 lb cooked
- 1 lb zucchini or butternut squash, optional
- julienned zest of ½ an orange
- julienned zest of ¼ of a lime - lemon ok in a pinch
- 2 packets Goya Sazon asafran, or other saffron bouillon
- 1 t salt (yes needed)
- 2 cups uncooked white or brown rice
- 4 large fresh or roasted red peppers, diced, 2 cups
- 1 bunch chopped scallions, green & white parts
- 1 bunch cilantro, about 2 cups chopped

VINAIGRETTE

- cooked, julienned zests from above
- ¾ cup orange juice
- 6 T lime juice
- 6 T white wine vinegar
- 1½ t ground cumin
- ½ t red pepper flakes
- 1 t salt

PREPARATION

- This recipes calls to use the same water for the corn, squash, zest and rice to retain nutrients and enhance flavor. This isn't required but is a great way to enhance flavor and nutrients in the salad.
- Cook corn covered 3 minutes in an inch of boiling water with ½ t sugar. Cool on a plate covered with a damp towel. Cut corn off cobs when it is cool enough to handle.
- Dice zucchini into ½" pieces and cook 1 minute - just to soften! - in same water with ½ t salt added.
- If using, boil or (even better) roast butternut.
- Cook zests for 2 minutes in same water - set aside for vinaigrette.
- Measure remaining water and add enough to make 2 ¾ cups for white rice, 3 ⅔ cups for brown rice Put back in pan with Sazon. Bring to a boil and add rice. Simmer 20 minutes (50-60 for brown rice) or until cooked.
- Fluff and let rice rest 10 minutes. If it is cooked and still watery, spread in a flat pan and let "dry" in a 325 oven for 10-20 minutes (and use less water next time).
- Chop remaining ingredients.
- Mix together vinaigrette.
- Pour ⅔ of the vinaigrette over the rice after it has cooled 30+ minutes, but is still warm. Mix in vegetables, meat and remaining vinaigrette once it is to room temperature
- Let rest at least 2 hours before eating.

Vietnamese Cabbage Salad (with Steak)

Vietnamese flavors are so fresh, clean and cooling. This salad demonstrates that perfectly. The original recipe is as a salad with steak. I like to make it that way and have included the marinade information, but I also just make the cabbage salad. If you have folks that don't like cilantro, though, you may want to omit it - or take some out for them. I served it at a picnic and had two very un-fussy eaters not like it because of the cilantro. Others raved about it!

INGREDIENTS FOR DRESSING - "GINGERED NUOC CHAM"

Makes 12-16 side servings

3 cloves garlic

1 large jalapeno

3-4 T peeled, chopped ginger (about a 2" piece)

2 T sugar

⅓ cup lime juice

¼ cup Asian fish sauce

THE SALAD

3 lbs cabbage, green and/or red

fresh (Thai) basil, enough for 1 cup leaves

fresh mint, enough for 1 cup leaves

fresh cilantro, enough for 1 cup leaves

4 cups mung bean sprouts

1½ cups chopped roasted lightly salted or unsalted peanuts

Kumquats on the table, if available

MEAT & MARINADE

3-4 lbs large sirloin steaks (or for your crowd size)

4 garlic coves

¼ c soy

2 T oil

SALAD PREP

• Make the salad dressing in a mini-processor. Grind the garlic, chile, ginger and sugar. Add the lime juice and fish sauce.

• Peel off tough outer leaves and quarter cabbage. Core and cut each quarter one more time lengthwise. Thinly slice or shred the cabbage and put into large bowl or rimmed platter.

• Wash and pat or spin dry the herbs. Pull off leaves to have 1 cup of each. Coarsely chop and stir into the cabbage along with the bean sprouts. Keep this refrigerated up to 3 hours. Otherwise wait to chop the herbs and add the bean sprouts.

• 20-30 minutes before serving, toss salad with ½ the dressing.

• Toss salad with the half the peanuts and rest of the dressing - or pass it separately.

• Sprinkle the remaining peanuts on top and serve.

STEAK PREP

• Coarsely chop the garlic. Combine with the soy and oil and marinate the steaks 1 hour - overnight.

• Discard marinade, salt and pepper steaks and grill to your liking.

• Thinly slice and serve on top of the cabbage salad.

Chili Cilantro Slaw with Grilled Fish

Once again-it helps to love cilantro. It is a very healthy herb. It has antioxidant, anti-inflammatory, and diuretic properties. Cilantro can also aid with digestion and the elimination of toxins from the body. Its pungent, citrusy flavor compliments the cabbage and fish in this recipe.

INGREDIENTS

Makes 3-4 cups slaw, about 6 servings

FOR THE SALAD

About 1 pound red or green cabbage (or a mix of both)

½ c thinly slivered red onion

FOR THE DRESSING/MARINADE

¾ cup cider vinegar

3 T extra-virgin olive oil

2 T sugar

⅓ cup chopped fresh cilantro

1 clove garlic, peeled and pressed or minced

1 t cumin seed

About ¾ t salt

5 to 6 t minced fresh jalapeño chilies

PREPARATION

- This recipe makes enough for the slaw and the fish. For just slaw, halve the dressing, or double the slaw or have leftover dressing.
- Plan to reinvigorate the seasonings after the slaw sits a few hours, or the next day.
- In a small bowl, mix the dressing ingredients and let sit while chopping the cabbage.
- Rinse and drain cabbage. Cut top to bottom into quarters; cut out and discard core sections.
- Chop the cabbage in a food processor using the thin slicer blade or by hand as described next.
- Slice each quarter in half lengthwise, then cut sections crosswise into thin shreds.
- Slice the onion very finely.
- In a large bowl, mix shredded cabbage, onion, and 1/2 of the dressing.
- Let rest at least 15 minutes. Remember to adjust seasoning to your taste.

FOR THE GRILLED FISH

6 6-oz pieces boned, skinned halibut or mahi-mahi

- Rinse fish and pat dry. In a zip-lock or Pyrex pan, combine fish, 2 T olive oil and ¼-⅓ cup of the marinade. Be sure to get it on all surfaces. Let stand, turning occasionally, for about 15 minutes (no longer or the vinegar will cook the fish).
- Start heating the grill (450ª F) after 7-8 minutes.
- Drain fish well and discard marinade. If desired, oil the grill at the spot each the fish will go. Place on a hot grill. Cook fish, turning once, until barely opaque but still moist-looking in center of thickest part (cut to test), 6 to 8 minutes.
- Mound slaw equally on the plates. Top mounds with a piece of fish. Pass remaining dressing if desired.

Purslane Potato Salad

Purslane is considered a garden "weed" almost everywhere in the United States, but it is a beloved wild leafy plant in Greece and Turkey. Make this salad in late spring/early summer, before the leaves get old and tough. This salad is best eaten warm, right away or within a few hours. If you wait, you may need to add more vinegar to brighten the flavors. This only keeps in the refrigerator for about two days, as the purslane wilts.

INGREDIENTS

Makes 6-8 Servings

24 oz golf ball-sized new potatoes (or larger in a pinch)

16 oz bunch of purslane; you need 1 ½ - 2 ½ cups of leaves
  Can substitute 6 oz baby arugula or spinach

½ c walnut pieces, toasted

2-3 T Meyer lemon olive oil or a flavorful extra virgin olive oil

3 T white wine vinegar (white vinegar is OK in a pinch)

½ t sea salt, more to taste

¼ t fresh ground pepper, more to taste

2-4 oz feta or chevre cheese, crumbled

PREPARATION

• Boil the potatoes whole in lightly salted water that just covers them for 15-35 minutes. (It's OK to put root vegetables in the pot when the water is cold.) The fresher the potato the quicker it will cook.

• As they cook, stem the purslane and carefully toast the walnuts in a sauté pan for 2-3 minutes.

• In the serving bowl, mix the oil, vinegar, salt & pepper and crumble in the feta cheese. Then add the purslane.

• Break the nuts into small pieces and add them.

• Once the potatoes are soft, pull them from the water and set aside in a colander to cool just a little.

• When they are still warm but you can touch them, half them (cut more if larger) and add to the salad. Eat as soon as you can!

Barley or Farro Waldorf Salad

COOK'S NOTES

• The grain will need time to cook and cool to at least warm before mixing into the salad. Cook up to three days ahead, cool at room temperature and refrigerate in a covered container.

• Make vinaigrette a day ahead if possible to give it time to meld.

• Spinach can replace the winter greens but it won't hold up as well if the salad is not consumed in a day. A little more can be added each time it is served, to "freshen" things up.

INGREDIENTS   *Makes 8-10 cups, serves 8-16*

FOR THE VINAIGRETTE

4 T extra virgin olive oil

2 T white or red wine vinegar

½ t sea salt

¼ t fresh ground black pepper

½ t sugar

2 T minced shallots, optional

FOR THE SALAD

1 ½ cups emmer or einkorn farro, or barley

3 oz walnuts, about ⅔ cup

12 oz apple, small chunks, about 2 cups

3-4 oz finely chopped escarole & frisse (4 cups) or 4 oz baby spinach

½ cup fine chop green onions, green & white

½ cup very finely sliced celery-optional

Seeds from a medium pomegranate or ½ cup dry cranberries, optional

2½ oz crumbled blue cheese, about ½ cup

PREPARATION

• Whisk together vinaigrette ingredients. If adding the shallots, let stand 15 minutes for them to soften.

• Cook the grain according to the package directions and let cool to warm.

• Toast walnuts for 2-3 minutes in a heavy skillet. Chop and add to a large bowl.

• Chop the vegetables and add to the bowl along with the blue cheese and nuts. Add ¼ cup of the dressing and stir to coat.

• Add the cooked farro/barley and stir gently with a large spoon.

• Season with additional salt and pepper to taste, and maybe even a squeeze of fresh lemon juice or a teaspoon more vinegar.

• Add more dressing, if you like, but you shouldn't need it all; save for another salad.

Mandarin Barley Salad

This beautiful salad is a close cousin to the Waldorf that precedes it. This was always a hit at my tennis team's holiday luncheon. It features the Satsuma mandarins that grace our backyard tree from December through February. Use an intensely flavored orange here or the flavor will get lost.

INGREDIENTS

Makes 10-12 cups, serves 12-16

FOR THE VINAIGRETTE

6 T Blood Orange Arbequina olive oil or similar

2 T Sherry wine vinegar

2 T Pomegranate Balsamic vinegar or similar

¾ t sea salt

⅓ t fresh ground black pepper

FOR THE SALAD

1 lb barley

1 cup pomegranate seeds (from 1 large pomegranate)

1½ cups sliced mandarin orange segments (3-4 fruits)

¾ cup roasted hazelnuts

¾ cup crumbled blue cheese, about 3 oz

1½ cups thin sliced endive leaves (about 3)

If desired, add green onions as in the Waldorf

Farro Pomegranate Salad

INGREDIENTS

Makes about 7 cups

1½ cups emmer farro or similar

½ cup roasted hazelnuts

1¼ cups pomegranate seeds, about 2 medium

1½ cups chopped orange

3 T minced parsley

1 T Pomegranate Balsamic or similar

PREPARATION

Try adding the Waldorf Vinaigrette to this salad.

WHOLE GRAIN COOKING NOTES

• I soak grains whenever I can. Even if it is just 30 minutes or an hour, this will cut down on cooking time. Soak refrigerated if longer than an hour.

• Don't stir the grains while they cook. As with rice, they will get mushy. If you feel the need to "mix it" a bit, just shake the pan gently.

Persimmon Wild Rice Salad

I was in New Jersey for Thanksgiving and packed a box of persimmons to share with my family and friends. We enjoyed this colorful, crunchy, sweet and savory salad on our Thanksgiving table. It is important to use the "Fuyu" (non-astringent) type of persimmons in order to get the "crunch". This recipe would make a wonderful entree salad topped with slices of cooked chicken, turkey, or duck. If you can't get persimmons, try substituting mandarin oranges, apples or crunchy pears.

PERSIMMON TYPES

- When purchasing persimmons, be aware that here are two types:

Astringent
These typically are a little more heart-shaped and need to be fully ripe and soft before eating, otherwise the tannins in the flesh are mouth-puckering bitter!

Non-Astringent
These are shaped more like a beefsteak tomato or a tiny squat pumpkin. They are lighter in color and can be eaten while still firm and crispy.

Either way, persimmons are an excellent source of fiber, Vitamin C, antioxidants, and minerals!

INGREDIENTS

DRESSING

1½ t grated tangerine or orange rind

1½ cup fresh tangerine or orange juice

Can substitute ½ cup concentrate - you won't need to boil it down

½ cup vegetable oil

¼ cup hazelnut or walnut oil - can substitute vegetable oil in a pinch

¼ cup white wine vinegar

1 t salt

¼ t cayenne

½ t ground cinnamon

½ t cardamom, can substitute ¼ t ginger

½ t coriander

SALAD

¾ cup raw brown rice, or substitute farro

¾ cup raw wild rice

1 head (12 oz) escarole - can use part frisse

1 large bunch watercress or 5 oz baby spinach

4 fuyu persimmons - the flat hard ones

½-⅔ cup hazelnuts, roasted if possible

Preparation and more Cook's Notes on next page . . .

PREPARATION

For the dressing:

- Boil juice in a small heavy saucepan over medium-high heat until reduced to 1/2 cup, about 15 minutes. Remove from heat.

- Let cool to warm and whisk in rest of ingredients. Adjust seasoning as needed.

Make the rice, combine the salad:

- Bring 3 1/2 cups water to a boil. Stir in 1 t salt or 2 t bouillon base. Turn off heat and add wild rice. Let sit 30 minutes.

- After 30 minutes, add the brown rice and simmer, covered, about 50 minutes. Once rice is cooked, turn off heat, fluff with a fork and let rest 10+ minutes uncovered.

- Rinse and dry the greens. Tear escarole / frisse into small pieces, discarding any tough white bases. Pick watercress leaves from stems and remove any large spinach stems. Roll in a tea towel to dry.

- Refrigerate up to 2 days in a plastic bag in a place where it won't get mashed.

- Slice persimmons into bite sized pieces - shape is your choosing. Could do some horizontal cross cuts for the top for a pretty presentation.

- If nuts are raw, toast them. See sidebar for methods. Chop as best you can.

- Place rice, greens and half the persimmon and nuts in large bowl. Add 6 T dressing and toss to coat.

- Add more dressing 1 T at a time, to taste.

- Divide salad among plates or put in serving bowl. Top with remaining persimmon and hazelnuts.

Summer Rice Salad with Cucumbers and Figs

This fresh, spicy & cool summer salad can make a main course lunch or sit happily on a buffet. Make it as shown, or have fun modifying it. For the meat and nuts, I used a leftover grilled pork chop and almonds.

INGREDIENTS

Serves 2 for lunch, or 4 as a side salad

2½ cups cooked brown rice

⅓ large cucumber, pinky nail sized chunks

4 figs, thumb nail size chunks

2 basil sprigs, leaves thinly chopped

12 sprigs cilantro leaves thinly chopped

Juice of ½ lime

2 T olive oil

1 ½ T good quality raspberry Balsamic vinegar, or similar

salt and pepper as needed

6 oz cooked pork, beef, chicken, shrimp, or tofu

¼ cup chopped nuts

1 T olive oil

2-3 T good quality raspberry Balsamic vinegar, or similar

4 shots hot sauce, or to taste

PREPARATION

- Combine the first group of ingredients. Add next group and stir in. Adjust to taste.

- Slice meat into julienne or to other preferred shape.

- Heat oil to medium high in a sauté pan. Add nuts and meat and sizzle 2-3 minutes, tossing twice.

- Add in vinegar and cook it off a minute to make a glaze.

- Put the rice salad on plates or in a serving bowl and top with the sauté.

COOK'S NOTES

- Using the proportions andquantities of each ingredient as a guideline, let what you have on hand, and what is freshest at the time, be the stars.

- Replace all but the rice in the first group with other fruits, vegetables and herbs. Try dried currants instead of figs.

- Try using farro instead of brown rice. Or use bulgur or couscous.

- Try lemon juice instead of the lime juice. Experiment with other aged Balsamic vinegars. There are so many available on the market today.

Warm Turkish Zucchini Salad

I am ALWAYS looking for more ways to use my zucchini crop. This is a new favorite - cool, creamy, lemony and sharp with garlic. The recipe comes from Clifford A .Wright's fantastic work, Little Foods of the Mediterranean. If you like simple foods unusually prepared and are interested in the culture and history of this region, this book deserves a place in your library.

INGREDIENTS

2 lbs zucchini cut into large bite chunks

1 T extra virgin olive oil

6 T full fat plain yogurt (if using low- or nonfat yogurt, double the oil)

2 garlic cloves, mashed

1-2 T lemon juice (about ½ lemon)

2 scallions, chopped

2 T fresh dill or mint or basil (or a combination)

½+ t sea salt

¼+ t pepper

OPTIONAL GARNISHES

Imported black olives

Sliced hard boiled eggs

Tomato chunks or slices

PREPARATION

• Combine yogurt, garlic, lemon, scallions, half the herbs salt & pepper in the bottom of the bowl you will serve or store the zucchini in.

• Cook zucchini covered in a wide sauté pan in ½" salted boiling water for 3 minutes at a boil.

• With a slotted spoon, remove zucchini to a colander to drain and cool a few minutes.

• Add it to the sauce and stir well. Mash the zucchini as desired. I prefer not to. Stir in the remaining herbs at serving.

• Enjoy this salad warm, at room temperature or cold. Flavors intensify with time, but the colors of the zucchini fade.

• Garnish if desired at serving.

* Inspired by Clifford A Wright (cwright@cliffordawright.com)

• Clifford Wright's version cooks the zucchini longer and mashes it (this is probably the traditional preparation). Plus his uses dill. Since I have more access to fresh basil and mint in the summer, I offer them as options. Each herb gives the salad a different slant.

Watermelon Tzatziki Salad with Cucumber and Mint

This dish is both refreshing and eye-catching. You will not be surprised to learn that Greeks have been eating watermelon like this (with yogurt and feta) for centuries. If the national watermelon growers association gets hold of this, they could double their annual sales!

INGREDIENTS

Makes approximately 8 servings (about 2 lbs)

2 medium cucumbers, 8-12 oz Armenian or Persian preferred, as they have fewer seeds

½-⅔ cup chopped mint

1 small garlic clove (optional)

1 cup plain Greek-style/thick creamy yogurt OR 16 oz yogurt, drained 1-6 hours (makes about a cup). See sidebar.

¼-½+ t sea salt

3 lbs. watermelon (makes about 6 cups chopped)

2 T fresh lime juice (1-2 limes)

2 T Meyer lemon olive oil or similar

NOTE: Proportions are approximate; A little more or less cucumber or watermelon won't hurt and is up to you.

PREPARATION

• Peel cucumber, halve lengthwise and seed. Coarsely grate into a medium bowl. Mash garlic to a paste with a pinch of salt (optional) and add to bowl. Chop mint and add ½ along with yogurt and salt. Mix gently.

• Chop watermelon into large bite pieces and set in a wide bowl. Keep everything cold until serving.

• Gently mix in ¼-⅓ of the yogurt sauce with the watermelon. Pour the rest in the center of over the top. Sprinkle with extra mint and drizzle on the lime juice & olive oil.

• Let guests serve themselves, taking as little or as much of yogurt part as they want.

• Option; add 1 or two peeled and chopped cucumbers in with the chopped watermelon.

MAKING YOGURT CHEESE

• This yields about 60%, meaning a quart of yogurt (4 cups) makes about 2¼-2½ cups.

• Set a 4 cup strainer into a bowl. Line the strainer with 2 or 3 thicknesses of dampened cheesecloth (rinse first if it's new). Spoon yogurt onto the cheesecloth, pulling up edges so it doesn't spill over. Cover with a lid or plastic wrap.

• Refrigerate, or if it is under 72º, leave on the counter. Let yogurt drain 6 hours - overnight, less if you want it still runny.

• Empty the liquidey whey if it touches the colander. It's good for cooking with soup or custard, if you want the tangy flavor.

• When it pulls away from the cheesecloth in almost one piece, it is done.

• To store, transfer to a clean container and refrigerate. It keeps as long as fresh yogurt.

• Rinse cheesecloth in several changes of water and a drop of soap until water is clear and cloth has no odor. Wring cloth and spread out to dry.

• Use this "yogurt cheese" in dips and sauces that call for sour cream, cream cheese (it's not as thick though) or crème fraiche.

Shredded Carrot Salad

This recipe is simplicity at its best — clean, fresh, good tasting, and good for you! Just 1/2 cup of carrots gives you nearly twice the average daily recommended amount of vitamin A, plus lots of valuable fiber! This salad goes with almost any meal, and is wonderful to find in the refrigerator when one needs a snack. Use the freshest carrots you can find, and try to buy organic!

INGREDIENTS

Makes 4-5 cups - 6-8 side servings

1½ lbs carrots, shredded

½ cup parsley, fine chop

⅓ cup scallion, fine chop white & green

VINAIGRETTE

3 T olive oil

2-4 T red wine vinegar

2-4 T lemon juice

2 t sugar

salt and pepper

PREPARATION

• This is best made 4-12 hours ahead of time.

• Shred the carrots in your machine of choice. Fine chop the parsley and green onions. Mix all three in a medium size bowl.

• Whisk vinaigrette ingredients in a small bowl - should be strong!

• Pour onto salad and adjust seasonings.

Gathering wild passion fruit on the island of Maui, Hawaii

69

Italian Melon Salad

This stuff can be addictive! Enjoy it in the summer or early fall when melons are flavorful and plentiful. Try out different varieties of melon. I always make a double batch as it is one of our favorite healthy, cooling, and flavor-packed snacks.

INGREDIENTS

Makes 4 good-sized servings

2¼ lb melon (makes about 1¼ lb usable)

1½ oz dry salami (secchi) - about 3 T

1 T chives, minced

1½ t white wine vinegar

1½ t fresh extra virgin olive oil

8 grinds pepper

6 grinds salt

Pinch red pepper flakes, optional

PREPARATION

• This can be made 2 -3 hours ahead. Store in the refrigerator... It is still delicious the next day.

• Chop melon into large bite sized pieces and put in the serving or storage bowl.

• Add the oil vinegar, salt and peppers and combine gently with a large slotted spoon.

• Slice the salami into thin matchsticks.

• Add half the chives and half the salami and stir again.

• Just before serving, sprinkle the remaining chives and salami on top and don't stir them in.

OPTIONAL AT SERVING

4-8 slices crusty bread

3-4 oz goat cheese at room temperature

• Toast the bread and spread with the goat cheese. Serve with the salad.

"Oh, this looks so yummy!"

Valencia Orange Salad

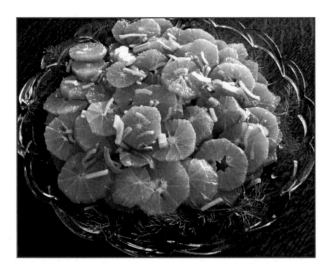

Unlike most citrus, my Valencia Orange tree yeilds ripe fruit in the late spring and early summer. It took us a few years to figure out when the fruit was actually ripe, because the tree flowers and sets the next year's fruit before the current crop is ready to pick!

After a trip to Spain and a fascination with paella, I discovered this recipe. We love it on hot summer nights. Plus, it is fun to take to parties as it is unusual and visually impressive, especially on a clear glass or dark plate.

INGREDIENTS   *Makes 6-8 servings on buffet, 4 regular*

FOR THE SALAD

4 large Valencia oranges

¼ cup 1" long julienne red onion slices

finely chopped fennel fronds or a fresh mint sprig for garnish, optional

FOR THE VINAIGRETTE

2 T white wine vinegar

2 T extra virgin olive oil

sea salt and fresh ground pepper

2 pinches of sugar

PREPARATION

• Mix up the vinaigrette.

• Fine slice the onion and put it in the vinaigrette.

• With a sharp knife, cut peel and white pith from oranges and slice horizontally into 6+ pieces. See sidebar for details.

• Lay orange slices on the platter and sprinkle with some of the onions. Spoon over a little of the vinaigrette. Keep adding layers and saucing.

• **IMPORTANT:** Refrigerate 45-90 minutes to let flavors meld.

• Mid-way through the melding, carefully pour the vinaigrette off the platter into a cup and re-spoon it over the oranges.

ENDIVE OPTION

• The salad can be served on a bed of endive leaves. Whole is more elegant, chopped is easier to eat.

• Prep the leaves from 1 or 2 endives to your liking and toss with some of the vinaigrette. Then spread onto platter. Top with orange slices, red onion and remaining vinaigrette.

• Or quarter the orange slices and toss with the chopped endives, vinaigrette and onion in a salad bowl. Marinate 20+ minutes.

ORANGE PEELING TIPS

• If you have a cutting board with a well or rim - as for meat juices - use it. Or, put a towel under the cutting board to catch the juice. Slice the top and bottom off the un-peeled orange so it sits flat.

• Hold the orange on the cutting board with one hand and carefully work the knife to take off a piece of the skin and white pith from top to bottom. Try to take about 1/8 to 1/6 of the orange. Go for more and you lose half the flesh.

• Do a first pass on all of the oranges, then do some cleanup. Switch to a small knife if you were using a large one.

• Carefully take off remaining big pieces of white.

• Now turn the orange on its side and slice thinly. A sharp knife is the key.

Hot Sweet Cucumber Salad

This is another of my favorite hot weather salads. The Southeast Asian "sweet-hot" flavor is so refreshing and palate clearing. I made 25 pounds of this for a friend's wedding and every bit of it was devoured!

INGREDIENTS

Makes 4 cups - 6-8 Servings

1½ lbs. cucumbers (use small firm ones or plan to seed them)

½ small red onion, about 2 oz

½ large sweet red pepper

1 jalapeno, optional

1 carrot

1 T chopped fresh cilantro

1 T chopped fresh mint

¼ c rice vinegar

2 T sugar

¼-½ t crushed red pepper

½ t salt

fresh ground white pepper to taste

PREPARATION

• Salad can be prepped ahead, but don't add vinaigrette more than 4 hours before serving as it makes TONS of juice. 30 minutes to an hour is perfect.

• Peel and chop cucumbers to your liking.

• Slice onion finely into 1" long pieces.

• Julienne pepper and carrot, also into 1" pieces.

• Chop cilantro and mint.

• If using, stem seed and remove white pith from jalapeno. Cut in quarters lengthwise. Slice crosswise as thinly as possible. Touch minimally (especially pith and seeds) to avoid a burning sensation. Wash hands with soap thoroughly.

• Combine vinegar and spices.

• Toss it all together within 1 hour of eating.

Crowd-Pleasing Appetizers & Dips

Beet Tartare

This dip is gorgeous in color and absolutely delicious. Sadly, many people will skip it at a big party, as they think they don't like beets. But just get them to try it and they'll never see beets in the same way again!

INGREDIENTS *Makes 2.5 cups*

1½ pounds raw beets, no tops

1 shallot, roughly chopped

4 T chopped parsley, divided in half

6 cornichons, roughly chopped

⅓ cup capers

1 t Worcestershire

1 t sherry vinegar

3 shots Tabasco or other hot pepper sauce

2 T mayonnaise (more if desired)

PREPARATION

• Scrub and cook beets - either by roasting or gently boiling. This step can be done up to 2 days ahead.

• To boil, put in a single layer in a heavy pan with a tight fitting lid. Fill with water that comes 3/4 of the way up the beets. Bring and keep at a gentle boil for 15-40 minutes. Check every 5 minutes after 15 minutes by gently poking with a knife. It should slide in with just a bit of pressure. Save the cooking water for making homemade broth, if desired.

• To roast, preheat oven to 375-425 (higher takes less time). Halve beets if large. Rub or spray all over with just a bit of olive oil. Roast, cut side down, on a parchment-lined tray until softened, 45 min-1 ¼ hours.

• Let beets cool 30-45 minutes.

• Roughly chop the shallot and put it in a food processor with the hot pepper sauce and 2 T of the parsley.

• When beets are soft and somewhat cooled, roughly chop and add to the processor. Blend to a coarse puree. DO NOT OVER PROCESS.

• Add mayonnaise, I T at a time and taste to check seasonings; it should have a bite.

• Sprinkle with remaining chopped parsley when serving.

• Serve with pita chips (best if you make your own), crostini, mild crackers, toasted baguette slices, or endive leaves.

Tepary Bean "Hummus"

The Tepary bean is native to the southwestern United States and Mexico, and has long been a staple food for many native americans. They come in a variety of colors- tan, white, golden, black, and speckled. Their sweet, nutty flavor makes them perfect for this delicious and nutritious dip.

INGREDIENTS

Makes 2 cups

¾ cup dry tepary beans
  (will make about 2 cups cooked)

2½ T fresh lemon juice

3 medium cloves garlic, coarse chopped

3 T extra virgin olive oil

¼ + t ground cumin

¼ t dried oregano + to garnish

salt to taste (⅛ + t)

OPTIONAL AT SERVING

pinch dried red pepper or paprika

minced fresh parsley or oregano

a drizzle of extra virgin olive oil

3 oz crumbled blue cheese

PREPARATION

- Cull and rinse beans. Soak refrigerated in 3 cups water for 8 hours or overnight.

- Cook beans covered at a simmer in about 5 cups water for 45-75 minutes. If desired, add a clove of garlic to the water for flavor. Save some, or all, of the cooking water.

- Once beans are cooked to your liking (for hummus they should be WELL cooked), add about ½ t salt to the water. Let beans cool.

- Puree beans and about 2 T of their cooking water, lemon juice, garlic, olive oil, cumin, and oregano until smooth.

- Save the rest of the cooking water for stock.

- Transfer pureed beans to a serving bowl and garnish as desired.

- Serve with crudités and/or pita bread or pita chips.

Marianne's Pantry product display

Chunky Carrot Dip or Salad

This recipe can be used as a salad, scooped on top of a bed of greens, in place of tuna or chicken salad. I prefer it as a dip for home-made pita chips for picnic lunches and just for snacking. It is really delicious, different - and good for you!

INGREDIENTS

Makes 3 cups

1½ pounds carrots, large chop

2 small cloves garlic, mashed

1 bunch scallions fine chopped green and white

2 stalks celery finely diced

1½ t dill weed; 1.5 T if fresh

1½ t fresh oregano chopped

2 t fresh basil - fine chop at last minute

4 T tahini

3-4 T soy sauce

1½ -2 T lemon juice, to taste

Fresh ground pepper to taste

PREPARATION

• Steam or boil the carrots in lightly salted and sugared water to just cover them until soft.

• As carrots cook, chop the herbs and vegetables.

• If the tahini is cold, put it in the microwave for 30 seconds. When the tahini is softened, add the herbs and other ingredients to it in a bowl that will hold the carrots too.

• Add cooked carrots to the bowl, reserving liquid for making soup stock later.

• Use a potato masher to combine everything.

• Add more lemon juice, herbs, pepper as needed.

• Serve with pita chips, endive leaves or scoop on top of fresh greens as a salad.

Roasted Grape Relish with Cheddar Crisps

I love finding savory ways to incorporate
fruits into my diet. This relish can be
served as an appetizer like tomato bruschetta,
on crackers or these delicious cheddar crisps.
It could also be served next to a piece of meat
on a dinner plate. The homemade cheddar
crisps smell heavenly when they come out of
the oven and melt in your mouth. Grapes are
naturally sweet, and become even more so
when roasted; if you prefer more salt or heat,
adjust ingredients accordingly. This unusual
recipe is always a big hit.

RELISH INGREDIENTS

Makes about 3 cups

1 lb seedless red grapes, off the
stems (3 -3 ½ cups)

¼ t salt

⅛ t black pepper

2+ T olive oil

⅔ cup pitted green olives

¼ cup finely chopped celery

¼ cup finely chopped red onion

1 t finely chopped fresh
jalapeño chile

½ t minced garlic

½ t finely grated fresh
orange zest

1 T red wine vinegar

⅓ cup toasted pine nuts

CHEDDAR CRISPS

*Makes about 12-15 crisps
depending on how deep you
make them*

1 cup coarsely grated extra-
sharp cheddar

½ cup all-purpose flour

⅛ t cayenne

2 T softened unsalted butter

PREPARATION

THE RELISH

- Toss grapes with salt, pepper, and 1 t oil in a bowl. If they are very
large, cut in half first.

- Spread on a parchment-lined baking tray. Roast at 400 until
caramelized and slightly shriveled, 25-45 minutes. Grapes can be
roasted up to 2 days ahead.

- While grapes are cooling, chop other vegetables. Toss cooled grapes
with everything else. Taste and adjust seasonings.

- Coarsely puree relish in a food processor or immersion blender.

- Let mixture rest 2 hours - overnight for flavors to meld.

- For best flavor, bring relish to room temperature before serving.

THE CHEDDAR CRISPS

- Crisps can be made up to 3 days ahead, cooled and kept in an
airtight container.

- Put oven rack in middle position and preheat to 400.

- Blend the cheddar, flour, and cayenne in a food processor until well
combined.

- Add butter and blend until dough starts to clump, about 30 seconds.
Turn out onto work surface and gently knead until well combined.

- Using palms of your hands, roll dough into a ¾-inch-thick rope
(should be about 24 inches long).

- Cut the rope into 24 equal pieces and press each into the bottom
and partly up the sides of a non-stick mini-muffin tin. If you use a
regular sized muffin tin, Roll your dough rope about 1" wide. You
will get fewer, larger crisps.

- Bake until golden and slightly puffed in centers, about 10 minutes.

- Cool in pan on a rack 10 minutes, then invert onto rack to cool
completely.

Green Bean Dip

This is one of the many vegetable spreads that we enjoy all summer long on our home made tortilla, baguette and pita "crackers". We'll have it with a weekend lunch, serve it as an appetizer at a party or dive into it when we are starved and dinner isn't ready yet. Its innate deliciousness makes it worth eating for that reason alone, but I see it as another opportunity to 'up' our fresh vegetable intake.

INGREDIENTS

Makes about 2½ cups

10-12 oz green beans

2 eggs, hard boiled

¼ cup walnuts or pistachios, toasted

½+ T olive oil

½ medium onion (about 3 oz)

1 clove garlic

2-3 T mayonnaise

1-2 T white wine or 1T lemon juice

¼ t sea salt & ¼ t black pepper, or to taste

2 T fresh chopped herbs, optional - use what you have, just not all one kind, except parsley

PREPARATION

- Hard boil eggs; Set in a small pan just covered with water. Bring to a boil, cover and cook, 10 minutes. Put in an ice water bath to cool. Peel and use, or refrigerate.

- Add green beans to 1" boiling salted water in a medium sauté pan and cook covered 3-4 minutes. Transfer to a colander, saving the water for soup stock.

- Toast walnuts (can do in the same pan).

- Mince and sauté onions & garlic (same pan). Season with salt and pepper as they soften.

- Coarsely chop the eggs and beans.

- Combine everything in a food processor.

- Adjust seasonings as needed.

COOK'S NOTES

- The eggs can be hard-boiled and the green beans cooked up to two days ahead. If doing all at once, use the same sauté pan for cooking the green beans, and then again to toast the nuts and sauté the onions.

- A food processor is needed.

- This benefits from having an hour or so for the flavors to meld. It can be made up to 8 hours ahead and keeps 2-4 days, refrigerated.

- Serve with simple whole grain crackers without a lot of added flavors, or better yet, make some homemade pita crisps.

Lunch in central market of Guanajuato, Mexico, 2010

Giant White Bean Dip

*M*ezzo Restaurant's Chef, Richard Hyman, was kind enough to use my Runner Cannelinis in a white bean bruschetta that he served at the Haggin Museum's May, 2012 Art A la Carte. It was so delicious that I decided to make a similar preparation to sample at the Festa Della Donna fundraiser a few days later. I served a single bean on a toothpick to the guests who came to our booth. The response was a collective swoon; plus we promptly sold every last runner cannelini that the grower had left! The dip can be served as an appetizer or a side dish, or a snack.

COOKS NOTES

• Runner Cannelini beans are an heirloom variety first cultivated in South America. They are widely used in Italian, Greek, and French cuisine. These big beautiful white beans have a buttery smooth texture and a rich nutty flavor. They are great in side-dishes, salads, and soups, and are delicious enough to stand all on their own.

INGREDIENTS

Makes about 3 cups - double the recipe for a crowd

½ lb Marianne's Runner Cannellini Beans or similar white bean

1 bay leaf

2 cloves garlic

2-3 T Meyer Lemon Olive Oil or other good quality fruity olive oil

½-1 t sea salt

¼-½ t fresh ground black pepper

¾ t dried thyme or 2 t fresh, minced

¾ t dried oregano or 2 t fresh, minced

PREPARATION

• Soak dry beans overnight in a cool place in 3+ cups water.

• Rinse beans and cook in a 1.5 quart pot with bay leaves, garlic and water to cover by 2". Partly cover the pan and gently boil until soft to the bite, about 75-90 minutes. If additional water is needed, boil before adding.

• Once the beans are cooked, drain off most of the water, leaving maybe ½ cup - I save it for making soups and stews.

• Add the seasonings while warm.

• Serve immediately or let cool and refrigerate overnight.

• Test seasonings and adjust as needed.

• The dip can be served as an appetizer or a side dish, or a snack.

Red Lentil Spinach Puffs with Date Plum Dipping Sauce

These are delicious and unique. A specialty in the northern and western parts of India, they can be enjoyed with a variety of sauces. These don't exactly puff, but this is the term used because the soaked (uncooked) lentils and baking powder leaven and "lighten" the batter. The sauce is also excellent on scallops and other seafood as a rub. The sauce in this photo was actually made with figs because I didn't have any prunes on hand. Serve the puffs warm and pass them around at a party and people will gobble them up!

COOK'S NOTES

- Lentils must soak 15 hours, or up to 3 days.

- Dipping sauce benefits from 4-6 hours to meld flavors.

- Food processor is needed for the puffs.

- Small blender, processor or "wand" works well for sauce.

- Mini (kid) spatula works well for flipping puffs.

- An electric griddle works great for this!

- If you don't have any dried prunes or fresh plums on hand, try figs for the sauce.

INGREDIENTS *Makes about 30-35 pieces*

THE PUFFS

¾ cup dried red lentils, soaked 16 hrs-3 days

2 t flour (rice flour is fine)

¾ t salt

⅛ t baking powder

0-3 T water

2 T coarsely chopped green onions

1 T packed, coarsely chopped cilantro

1 T chopped seeded serrano chile

1 garlic clove chopped

5 oz coarsely chopped fresh spinach

1-3 T peanut or olive oil for cooking

THE SAUCE

This makes about 1 cup which is plenty for a double batch of puffs. Use any extra as a sauce for scallops or other seafood (you might want to add a little olive oil).

4 pitted prunes, coarsely chopped (oil the knife)

4 large pitted dates, coarsely chopped (oil the knife)

2 T lemon juice, more to taste

½ t cumin

½ t ginger

¼-½ t salt

⅛ t red pepper

½ cup water (yes this much)

Preparation steps on next page . . .

PREPARATION

• Cull and wash lentils. Put in a 1 quart container with lid - they more than double! Cover with warm water 2 inches above lentils. Let sit at cool room temp (76 degrees or less). Refrigerate for at least 15 hours. Add water to keep them submerged.

THE SAUCE

• Puree all ingredients in a small blender or food processor or use an immersion blender. Thin if needed. Taste and adjust seasoning; it should have a punch.

• Bring sauce to room temperature or warm just a bit and serve with the puffs.

THE BATTER

• Batter can be made ahead of time, but must be kept refrigerated.

• Puffs themselves can be cooked ahead and reheated in a 250 degree oven for 12 minutes, lightly covered with foil.

• When lentils are ready, drain and add them along with next 4 ingredients to the bowl of a food processor. Use only as much water as needed - the longer the lentils have soaked, the less water they will need. Process until smooth.

• Remove lentils to bowl large enough to hold the rest of puff ingredients as well.

• Wipe out processor bowl and put the next five puff ingredients in and fine chop them.

• Fold this green mixture into lentil puree. Taste and add salt as needed.

• Heat 2-3 t oil on a non-stick griddle or sauté pan.

• Drop batter by teaspoon (or larger if preferred) onto hot oil. Let cook 4-5 minutes until golden on the bottom before turning and cooking another 3-4 minutes. Puffs will not spread so you can put them close together.

• Be sure they are cooked through not just golden on the outside - you may need to lower heat.

• Use more oil in pan as needed, but be sparing.

Biking with Dave in Yosemite National Park, 2007

Peach Salsa or Slices

This recipe came about because our peach tree was loaded with ripe fruit. We were eating huge portions of peach crisp every morning for breakfast and weren't making a dent in them. I modified a peach salsa recipe that I found, and made this dish for an upcoming catering event. I laid a single peach slice on each tortilla chip. This presentation was a big hit at Sorelle Winery's 2nd Anniversary party. I have also chopped the slices as for a salsa and served that with chips, and it was delicious. This dish is so versatile. You can also use it as a topping over grilled fish, serve it as a salad, or as a side.

COOK'S NOTES

- Make with other fruits depending on availability and whim - as long as it is flavorful.

- Adjust the heat to your personal taste.

- This doesn't need much time to "marinate", especially when really ripe fruit is used.

INGREDIENTS

Makes about 3 cups

1½ lbs whole ripe peaches (need 1¼ lbs after it is cut up)

2 T minced red onion

1 T minced mint

1 T minced cilantro (you could do all mint or all cilantro, or try some basil)

¼ cup good quality raspberry or other fruit infused vinegar

2 T Meyer lemon olive oil or similar

¼+ t cayenne pepper or red pepper flakes

PREPARATION

- Slice or small chop peaches according to your preference.

- Mince onion and herbs.

- Put all in a bowl and add vinegar, oil and cayenne.

- Stir gently. Let marinate 30 minutes - 4 hours. Stir gently occasionally.

- Serve with chips or as noted above.

Domata me Kopanisti - Roasted Tomato Blue Cheese Spread

*G*reece has been on my list of places to visit since college. A recipe like this only heightens my interest - simple, yet intense, fresh and delicious. I love tomato season! This recipe is great as a spread on bread, chips, on top of a burger or a chicken breast, or pasta or whatever...

INGREDIENTS

Makes 3 ½ - 4 cups (don't worry - it will get eaten!)

2 pounds ripe tomatoes; any size is fine

1 cup crumbled blue cheese, about 4 oz

½ cup crumbled feta, about 2 oz

1-3 T vodka or white rum, optional

2-6 T fresh flavorful olive oil

2 T chopped fresh mint

½ -1 t salt

¼ -½ t pepper

Pita bread or chips for serving

PREPARATION

• Preheat the oven to 375. Line a cookie tray with parchment or grease a glass lasagna pan.

• Core, halve and seed (seeding is optional, I don't) the tomatoes and set them cut side up on the tray.

• Bake for 1+ hour or until they shrink to half their original size. If the pan is really crowded, this could take almost 2 hours.

• Cool completely. If the tomatoes are still very liquidy, pour off and save for soup or rice.

• Coarsely chop the tomatoes by hand or in a processor. Drain off and save excess liquid.

• Mash the cheeses in a bowl. Gently stir in the tomatoes, 2 T vodka or rum, 2 T oil, half the mint, salt and pepper. Don't mix thoroughly. Taste and adjust seasonings.

• Everything above except the mint can be pulsed into the tomatoes, if desired.

• Stir in as much oil as desired without trying to fully incorporate it.

• To serve, scrape into a bowl and drizzle with oil and sprinkle with chopped mint.

COOK'S NOTES

• The tomatoes need to roast 1+ hour and cool fully, overnight if possible.

• The finished dip only gets better with time. Mix it all together 4 hours to a day ahead.

• A food processor or immersion blender can be used (gently), but is not required.

Caramelized Onion Tart

I love making this tart in late spring and early summer when our farmer's markets are full of locally grown onions. Yes there is a "season" for onions and yes, fresh ones really do taste better, at least I think they do. Onions are grown in most states, so check around and try for yourself. This tart can be served warm alongside or atop a salad as a lunch or as a first course for a fancy dinner. Or cut it into bite-sized pieces and serve as a finger food at picnics or parties.

COOK'S NOTES

• This tart, normally made in a round pie plate, works well to adapt to this rectangular style, as the filling is not runny. If the crust does flop over, just use a metal table knife or spoon to prop up the sides. Carefully remove the utensils right when you take the tart out of the oven.

• The dough needs time to chill. It is best to make it 2-72 hours ahead.

INGREDIENTS

Makes a 9" tart or about 30 appetizer bites

1½ cups flour

½ t salt

½ cup unsalted butter, cut into ½" cubes

½ c sour cream

heavy cream or egg yolk for brushing exposed crust, optional

SAUTÉ

3 T olive oil

3 large sweet onions (2 lbs), thinly sliced

2 t light brown sugar

½ t + salt

⅛ + t freshly ground pepper

2 T marsala sherry

1 t fresh chopped thyme (2 t if you triple recipe)

½ t fresh chopped rosemary (1 t if you triple recipe)

FILLING

¼ cup pine nuts (will toast)

1 large egg

½ cup ricotta

½ cup shredded asiago (or any kind), divided

PREPARATION

- Combine flour and salt in processor. Pulse to blend. With machine on, add butter and process just 6-8 seconds. Add sour cream and process just 4 more seconds.

- Transfer dough to board and finish mixing it quickly with hands (fraisage).

- Chill dough at least 30 minutes or up to 3 days.

- When ready to assemble tart, bring dough out of refrigerator and let it soften a bit as needed. Roll on a lightly floured surface to 1/8" thick. Flip the dough after every 3-4 strokes and roll from the center out only, rather than back and forth.

- Make a rectangle 7" wide and as long as you can get it. Fold over, then crimp up the edges and set it on a parchment lined cookie tray. If you prefer circles, try a 12" round shape in a pie pan.

- Refrigerate the prepared pastry until you fill it.

- Heat the oil in a large skillet over medium high heat.

- Add the onions and sauté, stirring often, until soft, 4-7 minutes. Add the sugar, salt, pepper.

- Reduce heat to low and cook, stirring often, until the onions are deeply browned and have a sticky texture, about 30 minutes.

- Add sherry and herbs. Cook 2 minutes more. Turn off heat.

- Preheat oven to 400. Position a rack in the center.

- As the oven preheats, put the pine nuts on a tray in the oven to toast 3-7 minutes. Watch carefully because they brown quickly! Chop them once they cool.

- In a small bowl, beat egg with the ricotta, HALF the shredded cheese, and the chopped nuts.

- Spread mixture onto the pastry and spread the onions on top, pushing them into the cheese.

- Sprinkle remaining cheese on top, and brush exposed edges of crust with egg white, if desired.

- Bake 35-40 minutes, until pastry is golden and filling sets. Let sit 10+ minutes before cutting.

The "Low-Table Café" moves to a streamside location

Stuffed Endive Boats

Stuffed endive are a visual delight, adding to any appetizer display. They are also great to pass around, so that you can explain the fillings. I made all four of these fillings for a cocktail party this April. We served them on pale pink glass trays lined with soft, airy fennel fronds. The guests loved trying all the different flavors.

INGREDIENTS

You get 7-12 usable leaves per endive

4-5 heads Belgian endive

4 T finely chopped herbs for garnish, optional

fennel fronds to decorate platter

recipe filling of your choice; suggestions below

PREPARATION

- Take endive leaves off the heads a couple of hours ahead. Trim them all to 2-3" long. Wrap in a damp towel and keep cool until use. Save ends and small centers for salads.

- Make filling.

- Prepare a platter or two with fennel fronds - parsley might work, too.

- At serving time, put 1 T filling on the pointed end of the endive.

- Sprinkle with a little chive, fennel or other herb if desired.

COOK'S PREP NOTES

- Assemble the boats just before serving.

- Do two flavors on a tray. Pass and let guests choose which one to try.

- Use the fronds of a fennel bulb to cover the platter. Then nest in the endives. This keeps each endive with filling from rolling around.

--- **FOUR DIFFERENT FILLINGS FOR ENDIVE** ---

🧂 SHRIMP SALAD

- If you can get the shrimp still frozen, do. Thaw 40 minutes before assembling by spreading on a baking tray. Dry thoroughly with a linen or cloth towel. Then mix them with the other ingredients. Otherwise they will give off water and make the salad runny.

1 lb cooked baby shrimp, drained and dry.

1 T chopped fresh tarragon

1 T chopped fresh chives

1 t Dijon mustard

5 T mayonnaise, preferably homemade

1-3 T lemon juice

1 t lemon peel

salt and pepper

more fillings next page . . .

BOB SPIEGEL'S BEET SALAD

1 T minced shallot

1½ T sherry vinegar

2-3 oz blue cheese, crumbled

12 oz beets, cooked, peeled and diced to 1/8 to ¼ "

¼ + t sea salt, to taste

⅛ t fresh ground pepper, to taste

- This filling can be made ahead. Just save half the cheese and stir it in at the last minute.

- Mix shallot and vinegar in a bowl and let sit for 10 minutes.

- Add oil, cheese, beets and stir gently.

- Salt and pepper to taste.

- **NOTE:** I went to grade school with a Bobby Spiegel, but I had no idea this was him until I recently ran into him at a high school reunion and learned he is a sought after NYC caterer.

TRUFFLED LENTIL & BLOOD ORANGE

1 cup green or beluga lentils - they hold their shape when cooked

1 T truffle oil -less is better; it "expands" with time

1 T orange zest

sea salt and fresh ground pepper

0-2 T white wine vinegar

2-3 blood oranges, or sub another juicy variety

- Cook lentils and drain. Season with salt, pepper and a wee bit of the oil while warm. Let rest overnight.

- The day of serving, zest and then segment the oranges, pull away the skin, and break into single segments or very small clumps.

- Mix in zest with bits of blood orange. Adjust seasonings.

- Add vinegar 1 t at a time if it needs a zing.

WALNUT PARMESAN

1 cup walnuts, toasted

1 clove garlic, minced

½ cup celery, minced

¼ cup chopped parsley

1 cup parmesan, shredded, about 4 oz

1 T mayonnaise

2 T lemon juice

2 T olive oil

salt and pepper to taste

- Toast and small chop the nuts.

- Mince the garlic and finely chop the celery and the parsley.

- Shred the cheese.

- Combine everything and season to taste.

Marianne's Pantry product display with huge pot of Paella

Caponata - Sicilian Eggplant Appetizer

My mom used to buy caponata in little cans titled "Sicilian Eggplant Appetizer". She took it to a party as a spread for crackers and the hostess raved about it. She said it was a "Family Recipe". It was a big joke to her because she usually cooked everything from scratch. There is something addictive about the agrodolce (bittersweet) flavor that comes from the combination of the vinegar and sugar.

SERVING IDEAS

- Italians eat this as a cold salad on lettuce leaves.

- It is fabulous on pita crisps as an appetizer. Spoon into a bowl and sprinkle with fresh chopped parsley.

- It can also be served on pasta or as a relish to roasted meats.

MODIFICATIONS

- Makes 1/3 recipe quite fine - doesn't take as long either.

- Any or all vegetables can be brushed with oil and grilled, if desired.

- Don't be afraid to mess with the proportions - the original recipe used no zucchini or bell peppers, only 1 cup tomato and 3 times the oil!

INGREDIENTS

Makes about 4 quarts (7 lbs or so)

¼ - ¾ cup olive oil

4 medium eggplants (about 4½ lbs)

4 large onions (about 2¼ lbs)

salt and pepper

4 celery ribs

1-2 each red & green pepper

2 lbs fresh tomatoes

2 large zucchini, 1½ lbs - or more eggplant

½ cup finely chopped parsley + more at serving

½ cup coarsely chopped basil + more at serving

½ cup capers, drained

2 t salt (approximate total to use)

1½ t pepper (approximate total to use)

⅓ cup red wine vinegar

2½ T sugar

1 t dried red pepper flakes

extra chopped parsley for serving

OPTIONAL ADD-INS

ripe black olives, pitted and chopped

pine nuts

raisins

PREPARATION

- Wash/rinse all the veggies.

- Peel and chop eggplant into 1-inch cubes.

- Sauté eggplants in heated oil in a heavy 6 quart pan in 2 batches with a lid on being patient. Adjust flame as needed so things cook and brown, but don't burn. Add a little water if it gets dry. Salt & pepper to taste after 5 minutes.

- Remove pieces to a bowl as they get golden.

- Meanwhile, chop onions into ¾ inch cubes.

- In a 6-12 quart stew pot, sauté onion with salt and pepper 5-7 minutes. Add oil as needed. Salt and pepper as they begin to soften.

- Finely chop the celery ribs. Chop peppers and tomatoes into one inch cubes.

- Add celery to onion and cook 3-5 minutes lid on.

- Once onions and celery are golden, add peppers, tomatoes, herbs, capers. Stir and cook 7-10 minutes lid on. Salt and pepper to taste after 5 minutes. Turn heat to medium if it is higher.

- Quarter zucchini lengthwise. Cut into ½" chunks.

- Once peppers start to soften and settle, add raw zucchini and cooked eggplant. If the pan is too full, add a bit at a time. Stir every 3 minutes and salt and pepper after 6-9 minutes. Cook 15 minutes with the lid on.

- Turn heat to low. Add sugar, vinegar and red pepper flakes (amount of red pepper will depend on your flakes and your taste buds).

- Cook 30-60 minutes, stirring every 7-10 minutes until well melded.

- Check seasonings after 30 minutes. Add salt, black or red pepper as desired.

- Use an immersion blender to coarsely purée, if serving the caponata as a spread.

- Add optional ingredients after blending.

- If you didn't use much oil in cooking, stir in 2-4 T good extra virgin olive oil once it cools.

Maianne and Dave picnic in Death Valley

Crab and Corn Stuffed Jalapeño Poppers

I've learned that I can't know which vegetables will give a bumper crop from year to year. After many pathetic pepper harvests, they recently became prolific - hence the development of a dish to use a lot of them. Cooking for 20 minutes virtually removes any overpowering heat from the peppers. Being that it is the middle of summer, I think the fresh corn is a wonderful addition. This is a standup cocktail party version of the classic pub fare!

INGREDIENTS

Makes 36-46 (depending on pepper size)

FOR THE CRAB CORN STUFFING

18-24 green jalapeños

8 oz can crab, drained

8 oz cream cheese

¾ cup chopped cooked corn

3 T fresh minced parsley

1 T other fresh herbs-optional

2 t lemon juice or dry sherry

OPTIONAL FINISHING ITEMS

3 red jalapeno for garnish

2-4 T olive oil

½ cup seasoned bread crumbs

½ cup semolina flour

¼ cup (about 1 oz) finely grated parmesan

PREPARATION

- Gently mix stuffing ingredients.
- Halve peppers lengthwise and remove seeds and pith - leave stem end in place.
- Stuff cored peppers and set on a parchment lined baking tray.
- Peppers can be covered and refrigerated up to 12 hrs.
- Can do one or two of the steps below before baking.
- Bake at 400° for 20-25 minutes until golden.

OPTIONAL FINISHING TOUCHES

- Julienne the red jalapenos and put a slice on top of each popper.
- When ready to cook, pour 2-3 T olive oil into a shallow bowl and half of each of the bread crumbs and semolina, into a pie plate.
- Dip pepper into oil and then roll in the crumb mix.
- Place close together on cookie tray.
- Add more oil and crumbs / semolina as needed
- Finely grate cheese over top if desired.

COOK'S NOTES

- I prefer stuffing the peppers from the top rather than halving them. In orer to keep them from leaking when cooking, I tilt them upwards along the edges of a metal pie plate, with a piece of onion in the center to prop them up.

- I like using thin-skinned, but spicy peppers that are fresh from my garden or the Farmer's Market. Fresh ingredients always have the best flavor!

Shrimp Corn Cakes

Recently harvested Brentwood corn and fresh, sustainable cooked baby shrimp from Oregon spawned this recipe. I prefer to add as little filler as possible to bind the cakes, so that the delicate flavors of the other ingredients can shine.

INGREDIENTS

Makes 8 big, or up to 30 bite-sized cakes

2 c cooked corn

1 lb cooked, well drained popcorn shrimp

4 scallions or ½ cup sprouts

1½ T parsley or basil

½ t sea salt

¼ t white or black pepper

2 T mayonnaise

1 egg, lightly beaten

6-8 T bread crumbs, preferably home made

flour to fry (¾ cup)

oil to fry

PREPARATION

• Puree corn - a hand salsa maker is perfect or a blander works. Small chop shrimp or add to salsa maker. Move to bowl.

• Gently mix in herbs, spices, mayonnaise with a rubber spatula.

• Carefully fold in egg with rubber spatula until mixture just clings together. Add bread crumbs as needed to bind it.

• Line a baking tray with parchment or wax paper. Shape each into chubby round cakes. Cover and chill at least 30 minutes (can refrigerate up to 24 hours or freeze 15-20 minutes).

• Put flour ¼ cup at a time in a pie tin or plate and shake to spread it. With a spatula, transfer 1-2 cakes (more if small) to the plate. Shake to spread the flour, then flip cakes with the spatula. Gently pick up each cake and pat it, letting excess flour fall off. Transfer these cakes directly to the heated pan or onto another parchment lined tray. Don't let them sit for long or flour will get absorbed. Add flour as needed.

• Gently lay cakes in skillet; pan-fry until outsides are crisp and browned, 4 to 5 minutes per side. Add oil as needed.

• Serve hot.

Wild Rice Pancakes with Apricots

I am always in search of wheat-free bite-sized appetizers. I'm not allergic or opposed to it, but I feel like wheat is everywhere, especially at "noshing" parties (and usually in a very refined format). Since I have access to wonderful brown and wild rice, direct from farmers, I came up with these tasty bites. They've made rave review appearances at two cocktail parties already!

INGREDIENTS *Makes about 50-60*

1 cup raw brown rice, about 1½ cups cooked

½ cup raw wild rice, about 1 cup cooked

½ cup minced dried apricot

½ cup minced red onion

¼ cup port wine

4 T orange juice (need another 3 T below)

2 t garam masala

6-8 T parsley

4+ shots pepper sauce or 1-3 minced jalapenos

1 T oil

1 t horseradish

½ t salt or to taste

3 eggs, beaten in a small bowl

1 T flour if needed

butter or oil for cooking pancakes

COOK'S NOTES

• Rice can be cooked ahead, cooled and refrigerated.

• The pancake mixture can be made ahead, up to adding the eggs. Do this just before using.

• Reheat leftover pancakes in a skillet with a little butter.

PREPARATION

• Cook the rice in lightly salted water. Cool to room temperature.

• In a small saucepan, combine apricots, onions, port and 4 T orange juice. Heat to a simmer and let sit at the lowest heat 10-15 minutes until liquid is gone and apricots and onions are soft.

• Gently mix this, rices and seasonings. Taste and adjust seasonings before adding egg.

• Beat eggs in a small bowl and add about ⅔ of the egg mixture. If it can take more, add it. If it is too runny, stir in the flour.

• Cook on an oiled griddle or in a non-stick pan. Use enough oil or butter to crisp but not saturate the cakes.

• Serve warm.

Zucchini Feta Pancakes

A perfect summer dish when zucchini is everywhere. The pancakes can be made small or entree-sized to fit your meal plan. They have a delicious delicate flavor that can be lost if served with an overpowering soup or entree. I suggest serving them as a first course or with other lightly flavored dishes.

INGREDIENTS   *Makes 16 big pancakes or 35 as finger food*

2 lbs zucchini, coarsely grated
  a mix of colors is great

1 t sea salt

3 eggs, separated

¾ cup chopped green onions

3 T fresh herbs such as mint, dill, sage,
  thyme, or parsley

¼ - ½ t ground white or black pepper

¾-1 cup crumbled feta cheese (4 oz)

½ cup wheat or spelt flour

Olive oil for cooking

COOK'S NOTES

• If zucchini are large, quarter lengthwise and cut out the seedy part. It is best to use smaller zucchini if possible. The zucchini need to sit 30-45 minutes after grating.

• An electric griddle or square pan is pretty much essential. It can be done in round pans but patience will be tested...

PREPARATION

• Shred zucchini and put in a colander set in a larger bowl. Toss with ½ t salt. Cover with plastic and set a heavy object on it (i.e. food processor base). Let stand 30+ minutes to drain juices.

• Separate the eggs, putting each part in a large bowl.

• Finely chop the green onions and herbs. Add with the spices to the yolks. Crumble in the feta cheese and mix well.

• After zucchini has drained, press on it, squeeze it between hands and/or squeeze in a linen tea towel to remove liquid. Save the liquid for stock.

• Beat egg whites to almost soft peaks.

• Preheat a griddle to 360°. If using stove top pans, preheat them to medium-medium high. If you plan to serve a crowd, preheat the oven to 275°.

• Add zucchini and flour to the yolk mixture and mix thoroughly. Fold in beaten egg whites.

• Lightly oil the heated pan(s). Begin making pancakes - ⅓ cupful makes a huge one, 1 T makes appetizer size. Let cook 3-5 minutes before attempting to flip. If they have not turned golden, give them a few more minutes; maybe turn heat up a little. Cook another 3-5 minutes on the other side.

• Place cooked pancakes on a cooling rack or cookie tray in the oven if you need to keep them warm. Do not over stack or they will get mushy.

Butternut Chevre Spread

Need a brilliant dish to bring to a holiday get together? This is it — easily made ahead, visually attractive, unusual, and delicious. It has a lovely color and an unexpected flavor. This spread is another way to get America eating more vegetables.

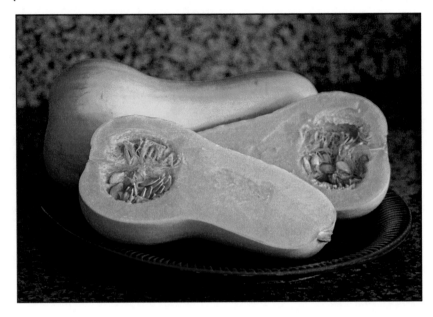

INGREDIENTS

Makes 2-2 ½ cups

1 medium butternut squash - 1½ lbs
1 whole head garlic
2-3 T lemon juice
½ t salt
tabasco to taste
3 oz goat cheese
¼ c chopped, toasted walnuts, optional
Baguette slices, crostini, pita for serving

PREPARATION

• Squash & garlic can be cooked up to 2 days ahead
• Spread is best prepared the day before eating
• Preheat oven to 400.
• Halve squash lengthwise; remove and discard seeds.
• Rub cut sides lightly with oil, and also the garlic. Place squash, cut side down, on a parchment lined tray. Wrap garlic in foil and set on tray
• Roast 40-60 minutes until garlic is golden and squash is tender.
• Cool slightly. Scoop out pulp and put in food processor. Squeeze out and add garlic "cream".
• Add lemon juice, salt and cheese to processor and run until mixture is smooth.
• Process patiently - it may take a few minutes. Season to taste.
• Let rest several hours- overnight for flavors to meld.
• Serve in wide serving dish. Sprinkle with nuts if desired.

Seasonal Vegetables

Vegetable Roasting Basics

Roasting does wonderful things to vegetables. It nicely browns them, tenderizes, takes away bitterness, and enhances their flavor. It is so easy to do and the result makes a great side dish, an easy to grab healthy snack, and a good soup base. Try dipping them in a garlicy Aioli (see recipe in Suaces chapter). Even picky vegetable eaters can be converted — guaranteed!

When roasting vegetables, be creative with different combinations, seasonings, toppings, and sauces, depending on your meal or your mood. I suggest a few ideas in the sidebar.

INGREDIENTS *Serves 4-7*

3 lbs raw vegetables

4½ T olive oil

4 T good quality thick balsamic vinegar (optional). Add 2-3 T more after roasting, if desired

1 t sea salt

½ t fresh ground black pepper

3 T fresh garlic, optional

3 T chopped fresh herbs, grated cheese, toasted nuts or seasoned breadcrumbs, optional

PREPARATION

- The three pounds of raw vegetables called for in this recipe will fill a 1½ quart serving dish once cooked.

- Preheat oven to 400.

- Peel vegetables, if desired, or if they are very large because skins or rinds can be tough. Cut vegetables into like-sized pieces or leave whole if small. See "Roasting Tips" below.

- Toss chopped vegetables in a big bowl with olive oil, balsamic vinegar (if using), sea salt and freshly ground black pepper.

- Spread vegetables in a single layer on a parchment-lined, rimmed cookie sheet or large roasting pan. Use multiple pans if needed. If the vegetables are stacked or too crowded, they will get mushy, not crispy and brown.

- Put in a hot oven. Check the tray(s) every 20 minutes. Turn the vegetables with a spatula and rotate the trays for even cooking. After 30 minutes, garlic may be added to the vegetables, if desired.

- Cook until the vegetables soften and brown. Enjoy as is or toss in fresh herbs or a little more balsamic.

ROASTING VARIATIONS

CUMIN-SCENTED CARROTS AND PARSNIPS

- Rub in 1 t cumin per 1½ lbs vegetables before baking.

TOASTED NUT CRUMB TOPPING

- Use sweet potatoes, potatoes, carrots, onions and Brussels sprouts.

- Toss the cooked vegetables with seasoned breadcrumbs (recipes on page 4, 29, 102, and 104), toasted nuts and fresh chopped parsley.

ROASTING TIPS

- Exact cooking time depends on the size, amount, and type of vegetables you are using. At first, don't mix multiple varieties on one tray.

- Root vegetables, unless chopped quite small, will take 45-60 minutes.

- Cauliflower, broccoli, Brussels sprouts, fennel and onion take 25 -40 minutes, or can be cooked at 375 for a longer time.

- Fresh whole green beans, asparagus and small carrots will take 25-40 minutes.

- Vegetables can be roasted at any temperature, but I like a 400 degree oven, or 375 if the vegetables are cut small and are very fresh. Going much hotter invites a blackened result. If the oven is at a lower temperature for something else, start them and turn up the heat when the other items are done.

- Remember - if you want crispy results, don't crowd the pan. A maximum of 2½-3 lbs of vegetables will fit on a large rimmed cookie tray. Smaller pans hold less.

Balsamic Roasted Asparagus

INGREDIENTS *Serves 2-4; double it if you love asparagus*

1 lb asparagus

1 T olive oil

2 t balsamic vinegar - a thick variety works best

¼ + t sea salt

fresh ground black pepper

1-2 garlic cloves, minced or pressed

2 t minced fresh tarragon or ⅔ t dried

PREPARATION

- Preheat oven to 400.

- Line a baking tray with parchment and spread the spears in a single layer, alternating spears tip & tail. Don't overcrowd. Figure on 2 lbs, at most, per large tray.

- Combine the other ingredients and pour over the asparagus. Use clean hands to rub the sauce all over.

- This can be done 10 minutes - 2 hours ahead.

- Bake 20-25 minutes. After 15 minutes, shake the pan and turn it 180 degrees. Swap trays top to bottom if you have more than one. Cooking time depends on the number of spears on the tray, your oven's actual temperature, and personal preference. The spears will continue to cook a little after they come out of the oven.

- If possible, let them rest 5-8 minutes in a warm place before serving.

- These are delicious to eat hot, warm, or at room temp.

MODIFICATIONS

- Use fresh lemon juice instead of the balsamic vinegar. Squeeze it on just before serving, rather than before baking.

- Sprinkle on some fresh ground parmesan after removing the spears from the oven.

- Asparagus can also be cooked on the grill - it takes about 10 minutes - maybe 15. Just rub the sauce on it, and then put the spears on a grill over medium high heat.

- Another option for the grill or oven is just to use salt, pepper and olive oil.

Roasted Brussels Sprouts with Apples and Almonds

Brussels sprouts sold in supermarkets are often picked too early, resulting in a bitter flavor and tougher texture. Try to find them fresh from local farms starting around October. Or better yet, grow them yourself! These little mini-cabbages are a cool weather crop and their flavor is actually enhanced after exposure to a couple of frosts.

INGREDIENTS

Makes 6+ side servings, less for veggie lovers

1½ lbs Brussels sprouts

1 tasty apple, quartered, cored and small chunked

⅓ cup raw almonds

½ cup thinly sliced red onion

2 T currants or raisins

3 T good quality thick balsamic vinegar

3 ⅓ T flavorful olive oil

1 t sea salt

¼ t fresh ground black pepper

⅛ t red pepper flakes

PREPARATION

• Set oven to 375.

• Halve or quarter larger sprouts; leave small ones whole. Chop apple, almond and onion smaller than the sprouts.

• Mix all in a bowl to coat. Spread to a single layer on a parchment lined tray.

• Bake about 40-50 minutes, checking and stirring every 10-15 minutes.

• Once cooked, taste. If desired, add a dash of salt or pepper, a drizzle of oil or balsamic.

COOK'S NOTES

• This recipe has many add-ins. I often leave out the almonds and raisins. But with everything, it is quite grand.

• Try to use a high quality barrel-aged balsamic vinegar that is thick and slightly sweet. If all you have is thinner, sharper balsamic, use much less.

Balsamic Roasted Roma Tomatoes
with Crostini & Lemon Cheese Spread

This makes wonderful "medallions of tomato" that can be used as suggested, or as a side dish to meats, or stirred into pasta or rice. It can also make a wonderful breakfast or brunch dish! Plum/Roma Tomatoes are perfect for this because of their low moisture content.

INGREDIENTS *Makes 36 appetizer servings*

THE LEMON CHEESE (OPTIONAL)

2 cups regular or goat yogurt

1 lemon

THE TOMATOES

8 oz onion very finely chopped

½ cup thick, mild balsamic vinegar

1 T red wine vinegar

2 T water or broth

¼ cup brown sugar

2 T olive oil

1 T grated ginger

18 small farm-fresh the farm Roma/plum tomatoes (about 1 ¾-2 lbs)

TO SERVE

1 whole grain baguette

OR use whole grain crackers

1 cup lemon cheese (that you've prepared)

8 fresh basil leaves

PREPARATION
THE LEMON CHEESE

- 1-2 days before serving, line a strainer with a double layer of cheesecloth and set in a bowl. Carefully pour yogurt into the cheesecloth.

- Grate the lemon skin and stir into the yogurt.

- Cover yogurt with cheesecloth edges. Top with a lid or plastic wrap and put in refrigerator.

- Drain liquid from the bowl after 2 or 3 hours and repeat two or three more times...

- Cheese should be done in 12+ hours. Transfer to storage container. It should peel right off when it is done. If you are in a rush, leave the cheese where it is and use the bits around the edges as they will be the thickest.

- Rinse cheese cloth in several changes of water and a drop of soap until water is clear and cloth has no odor. Wring cloth and spread out to dry.

COOK'S NOTES

- Cheese takes 12-24 hours to drain.

- Cheesecloth & strainer are needed for the cheese.

- Any type of flavorful tomato can be used, but non romas may take longer to cook as they have more moisture.

ROAST THE TOMATOES

- Combine first seven ingredients in a small sauce pan and gently boil 5-8 minutes.

- Set a regular (non-convection) oven to 400.

- Put whole tomatoes in pan(s) to determine correct pan size. Choose the one that is over ½ to ⅔ full.

- Core tomatoes and slice in half lengthwise. If using larger non-plum or really big tomatoes, then ¼ them.

- Put tomatoes cut side up in the baking dish in a single (very) packed layer. Some can lie a bit sideways

- If tomatoes are huge, put cut side down to start, and then flip them after 45 minutes.

- Pour sauce over tomatoes.

- Bake 1-1 ½ hours, basting every 20 minutes at first and every 10 minutes as sauce thickens. Non-romas may take longer.

- Be patient, but don't let it cook dry. Tomatoes are done when they are glazed dark brown and the sauce is syrupy. Sauce will thicken as it cools.

- Cool 40 minutes to overnight.

PREP THE BREAD

- Meanwhile slice the baguette into 36 or so pieces. Lay out on a parchment lined cookie tray.

- Bake 7-10 minutes. Bread should feel toasted and be a little browned. Bread can be also toasted on a skillet or grill.

TO SERVE

- Spread a little lemon cheese on the toasted bread.

- If desired, pull the skin off the tomato half and discard it. Put a tomato half on each lemon cheese crostini and press it in. If the tomato meats seem huge, cut in half. Put a few bits of onion on top.

- Just before serving, chiffonade the basil leaves and sprinkle over the toasts.

- Crostinis can be prepared a few minutes ahead, to allow flavors to soak into the bread.

Seasoned Steamed Artichokes

*T*he artichoke is an under-appreciated source of valuable health benefits. Most people don't realize that an equivalent sized serving of artichokes delivers more antioxidant power than cranberries or blueberries, and more fiber than peas, prunes, or raspberries. Fresh artichokes have a wonderful flavor, and if you are patient enough to prepare them properly, and get past the spiny leaves and hairy insides, you are rewarded with the soft tender heart meat.

INGREDIENTS

2-4 artichokes

1" water in the bottom of pan

1-2 T olive oil

4 T red or white wine vinegar

4 garlic cloves

4 bay leaves

1 t salt

12 black peppercorns

12 coriander seeds

½ t fennel or anise seeds

PREPARATION

• Put all ingredients, except chokes, into a large saucepan or 3+ quart soup pot with a tight fitting lid.

• Wash chokes, peel stem, remove several outer leaves, and slice off the top inch or so as needed to fit chokes in pot and have lid close. You can jam them in, but the lid needs to fit well or the water will evaporate too quickly.

• Bring covered pot to a boil; turn down to a gentle constant boil and let cook 35-50 minutes (up to 90 minutes for four huge ones) until tender. Allow 15 minutes more than you think you need. Undercooked artichokes are not tasty.

• As you remove artichokes, give them a gentle squeeze to get any liquid out.

SERVING IDEAS

• Serve with mayonnaise with lemon or mustard, and/or a little of the broth, or with butter and lemon. Make your own mayonnaise for a sublime experience!

• Pull open the leaves and spoon in about ⅔ cup cioppino or bruschetta sauce. Top with 2 T grated parmesan and 2 t herbed & seasoned chunky bread crumbs. Put in oven at 375 for 15 minutes to warm through.

Beets Pkhali

Such an unusual combination and it is delicious! Since walnuts are grown here in the Central Valley, I love finding recipes that include them as more than a "condiment". This dish is made throughout the Balkans, Russia and Turkey, where it is eaten on pita bread. Tweak as you wish. I serve it as a side dish and include pita.

INGREDIENTS

Serves 6 as a side dish

1½-2 lbs cooked beets

⅔ cup toasted walnuts

¼ - ⅓ cup chopped red or spring onion

1 clove garlic

3 T fresh cilantro

3 T fresh parsley

1½ T red wine vinegar

¼ t coriander

¼ t ground fenugreek

⅛-¼ t ground red pepper

¾ t salt, or to taste

pita bread (optional)

PREPARATION

- Gently oil whole beets and put in a single layer in a covered saucepan. Add water to come about ⅔ of the way up. Cook for about 45-90 minutes. Check for tenderness by pricking with a skewer.

- Slice whole beets into rounds, then slice the whole thing into thick matchsticks, then once more into cubes. Handle with care as the beets will want to slide around.

- Grind everything else with immersion blender or small food processor.

- Stir the mixture into the beets - it may seem strong at first but it will mellow.

- The dish is best if allowed time to meld flavors by refrigerating for 2 or more hours before serving. It will taste even better the next day!

Broccolini or Broccoli
with Balsamic Vinaigrette

Broccolini is a type of broccoli with long skinny "fingers", as opposed to the fat heads found in grocery stores. At the right time of year, the flavor and texture are absolutely wonderful. Whichever type of broccoli you use, try to find it fresh from small farms in your area. You will notice the difference.

INGREDIENTS

1½ lbs broccolini or broccoli

2+ T olive oil

1½ T high quality, thick balsamic vinegar

½ t Dijon mustard - optional

1 t minced garlic

½ t pepper

1 lemon, juiced at serving

PREPARATION

- Parboil the broccoli for 2 minutes in 1" of salted water.

- Combine other ingredients, except lemon, in small bowl.

- Drain broccoli well & put in a large bowl. Pour on sauce to taste. Add a squeeze of lemon and salt to taste.

COOK'S NOTES

- This recipe is very adaptable. Adjust proportions to your personal taste.

- This dish can be served warm or cold.

- A good quality balsamic vinegar should be thick and mild flavored. Most balsamic vinegars are thinner and have more bite as they are cut with a large proportion of red wine vinegar. You may want to use less of these.

Zucchini Gratin or Oven Fries

Here are a couple of delicious ways to use up those large zucchini that grow out of control in your garden, or that your friends have given you. I had one big 2½ lb Romanesco specimen and turned half of it into gratin and also made 36 fries. Just cut out the central seedy pith line that tends to exist in larger zucchini.

INGREDIENTS

Makes 3-4 servings per pound

THE VEGETABLES

2½-3 lbs zucchini (about 36 sticks)

⅔ cup aioli + more for the table (see recipe in "Sauces" chapter

OR use a mix of mayonnaise & pesto or other intense flavor, such as blue cheese crumbles

6-10 oz tomatoes, optional

THE BREADCRUMBS

6 oz fresh whole grain bread (need 3½+ cups toasted crumbs)

**can use semolina flour if short on bread crumbs

4 sprigs basil, small chop

3 T chives, small chop

3 T other fresh herbs, finely chopped, OR 3 t dried

4 T finely grated parmesan type cheese, optional

½ t sea salt & ¼ t red or black pepper

PREPARE BREADCRUMBS

- Put all ingredients into food processor. Pulse to process, but not to dust.
- Spread crumbs onto a parchment lined tray. Spray with Misto-type olive oil sprayer.
- Carefully toast at 350-375 for 10-12 minutes until just getting crispy. Or sauté in a pan with butter or oil for 3-5 minutes, watching carefully to avoid burning.

PREPARE ZUCCHINI

- Cut zucchini into giant steak fries; 4- 6" long and ½" wide at the outside. First cut the zucchini into desired lengths. Then cut each segment vertically in half. Slice again 1, 2, or 4 times depending on the size of the zucchini. If the seedy part seems pithy, cut it out.
- Parboil the "fries" in ½ inch of salted water in a covered pot, for just 3 minutes, to barely soften, or steam them. Spread a rack over a cooking tray to cool the zucchini.

FOR THE GRATIN

- Need about 6 T aioli for 1½ lbs. (See aioli recipe in "Sauces" chapter).
- Need about 6 T breadcrumbs for this amount.
- Can use any kind of zucchini - cut into steak fry pieces. Neatly (or not) spread the steamed sticks into the greased glass / ceramic pan.
- Rub most of the aioli onto the sticks. Salt & pepper.
- Finely chop the tomatoes and toss in the remaining aioli. Sprinkle artfully on top of the sticks. Salt & pepper to taste.
- Sprinkle crumbs over it all.
- Bake 20-30 min at 385-400. Can bake in a hotter oven for a shorter time, but watch closely to avoid burning the crumb topping.

continued on next page . . .

COOK'S NOTES

- The sticks are like "oven fries".

- They're delicious but a bit of work.

- The gratin is much easier and yummy also. You use about ½ of the aioli and bread crumbs on the gratin.

- A good method is to make enough sticks for the first night and a few for leftovers, then make the rest into a gratin and bake it. Enjoy that as a side dish for the next night or two.

- I like using a Misto oil sprayer in preparing this and other recipes. It produces a light, even mist of oil, which is nice, and helps you to cook healthier because you are using less oil.

FOR THE OVEN FRIES

- Put crumbs and aioli in separate pie pans.

- Put in 3-5 sticks at a time in the aioli.

- Use fork to move through sauce and then to crumbs.

- Use spoon to cover with crumbs and tongs to move to parchment coated cookie tray.

- Bake 10 minutes at 415.

- Spray sticks with Misto-type oil sprayer.

- Bake 6 minutes more.

- Or bake longer at lower temperature.

FOR THE SERVING SAUCE

- Finely chop the tomatoes and mix with remaining aioli. Tomatoes can be chopped in a food processor or blender, if desired. Salt and pepper to taste.

Hungry on the trail in Yosemite.

Sautéed Zucchini

In the middle of summer, everyone needs another great zucchini recipe. This is one of my favorite stand-bys. It is simple to make and doesn't require many ingredients.

INGREDIENTS

Makes 4 cups, 6-8 servings

1½ lbs small zucchini, yellow and or green

2 T olive oil

½ t sea salt

Fresh ground pepper

2 T fresh bread crumbs*

1 T butter (or more oil)

2 T small chopped shallots or red onion

4 T fresh chopped parsley or basil, or a mix of both

FOR TOASTED, SEASONED BREAD CRUMBS

1 slice of good bread, fresh or even better stale

1 T minced fresh herbs (or 1 t dried herbs in a pinch)

⅛ t sea salt and some fresh ground pepper

PREPARATION

• Halve or quarter zucchini lengthwise. If longer than 3-4", cut "sticks" in half lengthwise also.

• Heat the oil and cook zucchini on medium high for 5-8 minutes, stirring or tossing every two minutes. Salt and pepper to taste after 3-4 minutes.

• If they aren't softening, add 1-2 T water and put the lid on for 1-2 minutes.

• Once they just start to soften, add the bread crumbs, butter and shallots to the pan. Cook 1-3 minutes until the onions soften and crumbs are toasted.

• Toss in the parsley, turn off heat and serve.

MAKING THE BREAD CRUMBS

• Tear the bread into pieces and put into a spice grinder, blender or small food processor. Pulse until the desired consistency is reached.

• Fresh bread crumbs can be made ahead and kept indefinitely in a zipper lock bag in the freezer.

• For seasoned toasted bread crumbs, put ½-1 t olive oil per slice of bread in a pan and "sauté" the crumbs until they are crisp and golden, 3-6 minutes. Add salt and pepper to taste after 3 minutes and add herbs at the end. Store these in the same way as fresh crumbs.

Carrot "Souffle"

Freshly pulled carrots are wonderful any way you eat them. Here is a delicious treatment! Feel free to increase the ginger if desired.

Carrots are sold with their tops to show how fresh they are. Buy these when you have the option. Cut the tops off when you get home, as they pull the moisture from the carrots during storage.

INGREDIENTS

Serves 6-8 as a side dish

(This recipe exactly fills an 11 c. Cuisinart or a 1½ quart pan)

1½ lbs carrots – chopped, cooked

5-8 T melted butter

3 eggs

4 T unbleached white flour (can use ½ whole wheat)

1½ -2 T minced fresh ginger (or candied)

1- 1½ t vanilla extract

¼ t nutmeg

¾ t cinnamon

¼-½ t salt & same pepper

PREPARATION

• Coarse chop carrot. Put in a 3 quart saucepan and barely cover with water. Cover, bring to a boil and gently boil 10-25 minutes until carrots are soft. Drain carrots and save water for broth.

• Let carrots cool 10-15 minutes (or up to 2 days).

• Preheat oven to 350.

• Process carrots and rest of ingredients in food processor.

• For fluffier results, beat whites separately and fold in the carrot mixture

• Grease a 1½ qt pan and fill with custard, spreading evenly, especially at the edges.

• Bake at 350 covered for 45 min, uncovered 15 minutes more or at 375 for 45 minutes uncovered.

Winter Squash Bake

There are many varieties of squash put into the "winter" category, including Acorn, Butternut, Hubbard, Delicata, Pumpkin, and others. Find what looks good and be adventurous. This makes an easy and delicious casserole with many healthy ingredients.

INGREDIENTS

Serves 10 as a side, 8 for big eaters

2 lbs winter squash, peeled & cubed

2 cups salted water or broth

2-3 T butter, divided

¾ cup onions, chopped

½ cup celery, thinly sliced

½ cup walnuts

⅔ cup cranberries

½ cup white wine

1 cup apples, small chunks or slices

1½ T fresh sage

1½ T fresh thyme

½ t Five Spice blend

2 T grated orange peel, optional

2 T maple syrup, apple cider, or orange juice

PREPARATION

• Parboil squash cubes 5-7 minutes until just softening in water - save liquid for soup. *Don't cook too much!*

• Sear onions and celery in 1-2 T butter or oil. Salt and pepper to taste and add walnuts. Cook 3 minutes. Add cranberries and wine and stir. Cook to lose ½ the liquid.

• Toss hot squash and remaining ingredients in the sauté pan if they fit, or in a large bowl. Add the sauteed mix.

• Transfer to a buttered 13x9" pan. Put small bits of 1 T of the remaining butter over top or dribble with 1 T olive oil.

• Bake at 400 for 30-45 minutes.

Balsamic Braised Chard or Collard Greens

This is a wonderful recipe base for preparing winter greens. Agrodolce, literally "agro" (sour) and "dolce" (sweet), is a classic Italian flavor combination. Use dried fruit and nuts as you wish, or use none. Just use fresh greens and you will love the results!

INGREDIENTS

2 lbs Swiss chard or collard greens

8 oz red onion

3 T olive oil

3 T chopped pecans or pine nuts (optional)

salt and pepper

2 cloves garlic mashed

3 T balsamic vinegar

1+ T brown sugar

2-4 T dried cherries or golden raisins

PREPARATION

• Wash greens well

• Remove stems from greens. Chop leaf part well. Toss all collard ends. Toss ½ of the chard ends. Fine chop the rest. Keep separate from leaves.

• Fine slice the onion.

• Heat the oil to medium-high. Add onion and chard bottoms and cook 3-5 minutes until they just begin to soften.

• Add the nuts, salt and pepper and keep cooking three minutes.

• Add the garlic and cook one minute.

• Add the chard and remaining ingredients. Toss to coat 1-2 minutes. Cover and turn down to medium or medium-low. Cook 5-15 minutes until greens are to your liking. Season more, as needed.

MODIFICATIONS

• Add 2-4 oz. bacon to the onion sauté.

• Use cider vinegar, 1 T honey, no nuts or gold raisins.

• Add 4 T chopped fresh mint; 2 T to sauté and 2 T at serving.

COOK'S NOTES

• Shake greens well and let rest in a colander to drain off excess water.

• If the greens seem really dirty, rinse them again after chopping. Again, drain well, even roll in a linen towel or cloth napkin to remove extra water before cooking.

• Collard greens need to cook for a much longer time than chard.

Grilled Eggplant and Zucchini

Ok - so I cheated and used a photo of zucchini; the eggplant will look just as delicious. But, why not grill some zucchini at the same time? They don't need to be salted, so they are quicker to prepare.

This dish is so easy to make, and so good. It can be eaten hot, at room temperature or cold. Any number of sauces can be put on the grilled eggplant and it can be enjoyed as a side dish or a snack. Or, slice the eggplant up and put it in a salad or on pasta. Melt some cheese on a slice of grilled eggplant and put it into a sandwich. The possibilities are endless.

INGREDIENTS

Fresh eggplants (or zucchini)

Olive oil

Sea salt and fresh ground pepper

Finishing sauce of your choice - see ideas below

PREPARATION

• Peel off skin of eggplant in stripes - both for decoration and to make it easier to bite. Slice into ½ inch pieces, lengthwise or crosswise.

This next step is optional, but many cooks that I highly respect recommend this, so I now always fit it in.If using zucchini instead of eggplant, this step does not apply.

• Lay eggplant slices on a tray lined with paper or a linen towel. Some can be touching but not overlapping. Sprinkle both sides of the slices with salt. Lay another towel on top. Allow the eggplant to rest and drain like this for 30 minutes. The salt will pull bitter juices out of the eggplant. Rinse off excess salt, then pat dry with paper towels.

• Light the grill.

• Lightly oil both sides of the dried eggplants with a basting brush or Misto type oil sprayer.

• Salt and pepper both sides.

• Grill 2-4 minutes per side.

• Remove from grill and baste with the sauce of your choice.

SAUCE IDEAS

• Any type of pesto or chutney or salsa

• Good balsamic vinegar and olive oil

• The above with some crumbled chevre or blue cheese - or shavings of parmesan.

• A mix of mashed garlic, olive oil and fresh herbs salt, red chili flakes and black pepper

Sautéed Green Beans with Shallots and Tarragon

These are so simple and so good. Enjoy this recipe as is or use as a base recipe and, change the herb, add nuts or lemon zest, or prosciutto. We never tire of green beans when they are in season, which for us is late May - October. Yum!

INGREDIENTS

Makes 4- 6 servings

1 lb beans, stem end trimmed

1-1 ½ T butter

2 T minced shallots or red onion

1-2 T finely chopped fresh tarragon, or 1-2 t dried

½ t sea salt

freshly ground pepper to taste

PREPARATION

- The beans can be parboiled up to a day ahead. Once cooked, spread on a rimmed baking tray to cool them. If using later, cover with ice to quickly cool and retain color. Drain well, and refrigerate in a lidded container if it will be more than an hour or so until use.

- Heat ¾" salted water in a wide sauté pan that has a lid. When it comes to a boil, leave the heat on high, add the beans and cook 3 minutes.

- Save cooking water for stock and put the beans in a colander or spread on a tray as described above. Put a few ice cubes on top, if you have some.

- Sauté the shallots in butter in that same pan. Lightly salt and pepper after a couple of minutes. This can also be done ahead of time.

- When ready to eat, reheat the shallots.

- Add the cooked, drained beans. Toss with the shallots to heat and cook to your desired tenderness. If the beans don't seem to be cooked to your taste, add a little water (2-3 T), put a lid on and cook a couple of minutes more.

- Add tarragon and salt and pepper to taste and cook another 30 seconds.

Thai Green Beans

Beans are considered unripe fruit since they are picked and eaten before the seeds inside have fully matured. I could eat them 3 times a week! Here's another yummy, and healthy, idea.

INGREDIENTS

1½ lbs green beans

1 T peanut or canola oil

2 cups sliced mushrooms

6 cloves minced garlic

½ small onion cut into thin slivers, optional

1½ T soy sauce

½ t Asian chili sauce or red pepper flakes to taste

1 T white wine

¼ cup roasted peanuts

4 sliced scallions

2 T chopped fresh cilantro

PREPARATION

• Bring about ½-¾" salted water to a boil in a lidded sauté pan. Cut the beans into 1-2" pieces and cook for 4 minutes. Remove them to a colander and save cooking water for stock.

• Wipe out pan and heat oil in it. Add the mushrooms and onions and cook 3-4 minutes on medium high.

• Once they begin to soften, add the garlic, soy and chile. Cook 2 minutes more until they are almost done and add back the beans and the wine. Keep the heat high to sizzling and toss everything to mix well.

• Add the peanuts and toss another minute. Finally add the scallions and cilantro. Adjust seasonings, serve and enjoy.

COOK'S NOTES

• Try adding other traditional Thai ingredients such as thinly sliced lemongrass, or some chopped Thai basil, or garnish with some toasted coconut.

Kohlrabi / Mushroom Puree

I am always looking to expand my repertoire of vegetables that we eat. In years past, I bought bulbs of Kohlrabi and stared at them until I gave up. I recall slicing and sautéing some once and not being excited. I tried putting them in a salad, with little delight. However, this recipe changed things for me. I now jump on kohlrabi when I see fresh ones — the leaves are still on and are green and sprightly, and I like them the size of a tennis ball, not a softball.

Kohlrabi tastes like a nutty, sweet variant of broccoli stems. The bulb can be eaten raw or cooked, but the leaves should be cooked. Store them refrigerated in a brown paper bag, inside a plastic, bag for 7-10 days. You might cut off the leaves and gently roll them in a linen towel/cloth napkin and store in their own plastic bag, to avoid their getting squished.

INGREDIENTS *Makes 6-8 servings*

2½ lbs kohlrabi bulbs with leaves

1+ T butter

1 8-10 oz onion, chopped, about 2 cups

3 cloves garlic, minced

4-5 oz mushrooms, sliced

4-6+ T creme friache OR cream, milk, chicken stock

½ -1 T lemon juice

sea salt and freshly ground pepper to taste

PREPARATION

- A food processor is ideal but a sturdy blender works; the latter may require extra cooking water and/or processing in batches.

- Set a 3 quart pan with 2" of water on to boil. Add 1 + t salt.

- Carefully trim and peel the kohlrabi bulbs. Discard any woody parts and yellow leaves. Coarsely chop the rest into about ½ x1" chunks.

- Once the water boils, add the chunks. Set the leaves aside. Reduce the heat and simmer, covered, until tender, 15-20 minutes.

- Meanwhile, heat the butter in a skillet. Add the onion and sauté over medium-low until softened, about 5 minutes. Finely chop any thick parts of the kohlrabi leaf stems and add to the skillet. Add the garlic and mushrooms and cook, stirring, 5-7 minutes over medium-low heat. Do not let things brown. If the mixture is dry, add more butter or 1+T of the kohlrabi cooking water.

- Add the kohlrabi leaves to the skillet. Cover, and cook 5 minutes. Uncover, and cook, stirring, until all the liquid has evaporated, 1-3 minutes.

- Drain the kohlrabi chunks and place in the bowl of a food processor. Save the water for stock. Add the mushroom mixture and the remaining ingredients. Purée until smooth.

- If needed, transfer purée to a saucepan and reheat over low heat.

Spaghetti Squash—Two Ways

ike other winter squash, spaghetti squash are grown over the summer and harvested in the fall. They keep well in cool dark storage, so can be enjoyed over the winter, hence the term :winter" squash.

Unlike other squash, they have tender, stringy, mild-tasting meat inside. Spaghetti squash is great for people on low carb or gluten-free diets because you can pretend it is spaghetti, while you're really eating a vegetable.

PREPARATION — JUST THE SQUASH

• This can be done up to a day ahead.

• Bake at 375 for 1 hour or microwave it 15-20 minutes. Halve it lengthwise and remove the seeds before you cook it or remove them after cooking. I do this before and cook the halves cut side down on a parchment-lined tray.

• Let squash cool 30+ minutes before handling. When cool, use a fork or fingers to pull the spaghetti strands away from the sides of the squash and tease them apart.

■ *Basic*

1 spaghetti squash, about 2 pounds

1-2 T butter

sea salt and freshly ground pepper

parmesan cheese

parsley or other fresh herbs

• Bake squash as above.

• Warm some butter and add to the "spaghettis".

• Salt and pepper to taste and heat through.

• Sprinkle on some parmesan cheese, parsley.

■ *Simple Tomato Casserole*

1 spaghetti squash, about 2 pounds

28 oz can Italian style stewed or whole tomatoes

2-6 T ricotta, chevre or blended cottage cheese

⅓ cup grated parmesan (about 1½ oz)

sea salt and freshly ground pepper

parmesan cheese

2 T parsley or other fresh herbs if available

• Bake squash as above.

• Heat oven to 350-375.

• Choose temperature and cooking time to fit your schedule.

• Lightly oil a 3 qt oven-safe dish.

• If using fresh tomatoes, sauté and stew down for about 45 minutes. Season with salt, pepper, garlic, and herbs.

• Chop the parsley.

• Combine the shredded spaghetti squash, tomatoes, parsley, ricotta and 2 T of the parmesan cheese. Stir to mix.

• Sprinkle the remaining parmesan on top.

• Bake at 350-375 for 20-40 minutes until bubbly and cheese is browned.

Spaghetti Squash Bake (Kitchen Sink)

This is a delicious one-dish, make-ahead meal, with Mediterranean overtones. It is similar to the Simple Tomato Casserole on the previous page, but heartier, with the addition of meat, and more cheese and veggies. Serve with a salad or pair with green vegetables or meat.

Ingredients are variable. Use what you like or have on hand. Just remember to use flavorful ingredients and season everything well.

If you're in the mood for Greek instead of Italian, use feta and another Greek cheese, and add olives and pepperoncini, with ground lamb or Greek sausage.

INGREDIENTS

Makes a 2 quart pan (5-8 servings)

1 spaghetti squash

1-3 T olive oil

1 medium onion, 8-10 oz

8-12 oz sausage, optional

2-3 cloves garlic

1 fresh or roasted pepper

1 small zucchini

8 oz mushrooms

2 T fresh (2 t dried) mixed Italian herbs - oregano, thyme, marjoram, parsley

1 t fennel seeds

28 oz can Italian style stewed or whole tomatoes

8-12 oz ricotta, chevre, or mozzarella; can substitute with sour cream or blended cottage cheese

1 cup grated parmesan

sea salt and fresh ground pepper

PREPARATION

• Bake the squash as described in the previous recipe page.

• Chop the vegetables small for the tomato sauce.

• Heat olive oil in a 4 quart stock pot or sauté pan. Add onion and sausage to pot and sauté on medium to medium-high heat for 3-5 minutes until onion begins to soften. Add salt and pepper to taste.

• Add pepper, if it is raw, and mushrooms. Add zucchini after mushrooms soften. Cook 5 more minutes. Salt and pepper to taste. Drain if really greasy.

• Return to heat and add ⅓ cup red wine and cook it off. Add tomatoes, half the Italian herbs and all of the fennel.

• Simmer 40 minutes, stirring 4-5 times.

• Meanwhile, shred cooked "spaghettis" into a large bowl. Combine with ¾ of the sauce, the soft cheese and about ½ of the parmesan, the rest of the herbs, salt and pepper to taste.

• Pour mixture into a greased 2 quart oven-proof dish. Bake covered at 375 for 30 minutes (until bubbling), then uncovered 10-15 minutes to color the cheese and crisp the top. Can broil if preferred.

• Sprinkle with remaining parmesan at serving, if desired.

Hearty Grains, Pastas & Beans

Cooking with Farro

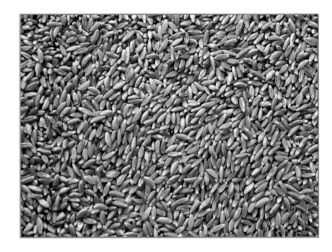

*F*arro is the ancient grandparent of today's wheat. It originated in the Fertile Crescent of the Middle East, and has been found in the tombs of Egyptian Kings. It has an earthy, nutty taste and a cushiony texture that kind of "pops" in your mouth as you chew. It is delicious in savory dishes for dinner sides and salads or sweetened for breakfast.

There are actually three types of farro; einkorn (piccolo), emmer (medio) and spelt (grande), which roughly refer to the relative sizes of the grains. Einkorn and emmer farro grains have not been industrialized or genetically modified as the younger wheat has been. Farro is considerably higher in protein and lower in gluten than today's wheat, and it is generally more easily digestible. The bran, where minerals, vitamins and antioxidants are found, is thicker on farro grains than on wheat. The Italians employ a process called "pearling" which reduces cooking time by removing some of the bran. You actually see a white strip around the center of the grain of pearled farro, where the bran and much of its nutritional goodness have been stripped away. That is why I prefer to cook with unpearled farro.

COOK'S NOTES

- Soaking farro for 1-5 hours before cooking will reduce the amount of time required for cooking. Put in the amount of water or broth that you would eventually use for cooking and don't rinse it when it's time to cook.

- If you don't soak the farro ahead of time, I suggest toasting it in a dry sauté pan for about 5 minutes over medium heat, shaking often. This will enhance flavor and reduce cooking time a little.

- Farro can be made ahead. Let it cool with any extra cooking liquid.

BASIC INGREDIENTS

Makes about 2¼ cups, 3-4 servings

1 cup einkorn or emmer farro

2 c water or 1¾ c broth

½ + t sea salt

BASIC POT OF FARRO PREPARATION

- Use a pan with tight fitting lid.

- Add water or broth to farro. If broth is unsalted add ½ t salt.

- Cover and bring to a gentle boil. Simmer about an hour for emmer, 40-50 minutes for einkorn.

- Let farro cool in the pan with any extra water if using the next day.

- Otherwise, proceed with your desired recipe.

- If you are planning to eat it as is, season as desired with herbs, pepper and a little olive oil.

- A squeeze of citrus or a grating of parmesan would also be delicious.

Jazzed-up Farro #1

Makes about 4 cups, 5-8 servings

• This is a very loose offering. Change up ingredients to fit your fancy and what's in your pantry.

8 oz onion

8 oz mushroom

8 oz kale or chard, beet greens etc...

4 cloves garlic

sea salt and fresh ground pepper to taste

• Prepare farro as in A Basic Pot of Farro recipe.

• While it cooks, sauté the above ingredients. Season with salt and pepper to taste. Add herbs as available.

• Once the farro is cooked, stir in sautéed ingredients and let the dish rest 2-3 minutes before serving.

Jazzed-up Farro #2

Makes about 3.75 cups, 4-7 servings

• This recipe goes wonderfully with Greek and other Mediterranean meals. I developed it to accompany a kale and mushroom moussaka for a women's ski trip.

• The cheese is optional. Omit if this is being served with an already rich meal like moussaka.

• If desired or appropriate, make the farro ahead, make the sauté ahead, combine them and reheat in the oven. Top with the feta at serving, if using.

⅓ cup walnuts, toasted and chopped (or pine nuts)

1 medium-sized red onion (about 1½ cups minced)

1 T fruity olive oil

sea salt and fresh ground pepper to taste

2 T white wine

⅓ cup currants

⅓ cup feta, optional

• Prepare farro following Basic Pot of Farro recipe.

• This can be done up to two days ahead. Store covered in the refrigerator.

• While the farro cooks, toast walnuts 3-4 minutes over medium heat. Let cool and chop to a small size.

• Mince the onion and sauté in the same pan the walnuts were in. Salt and pepper once they soften. Add the wine and the currants and turn heat to low. Let meld 3-5 minutes until wine is mostly absorbed.

• Add the farro along with any remaining cooking water and stir gently to combine. Let the farro heat up and steam for 10 or so minutes. If the pan is really dry, add a little water.

• You can't really overcook farro, but it can burn to the bottom of the pan, so watch the heat.

Risotto -vs- Farrotto with Porcini Mushrooms

■ Risotto

Ever since I discovered Carnaroli rice, I love to make risottos. It is sometimes referred to as the "Caviar of rice" because of its delicious flavor and creamy texture. This rice makes perfect al dente risotto every time. Carnaroli rice was the start of my pantry business and I absolutely love how it cooks up. This recipe features my unorthodox way of making risotto that I find to be foolproof and totally stress free. The traditional method directions are included as well, if you prefer.

■ Farrotto

Since I love cooking with farro, I have tried it in a lot of recipes, and discovered it makes a good, hearty untraditional risotto, or I should say "farotto". It's not quite as soft as the classic northern Italian risotto made with Carnaroli or arborio rice, but with the cheese, wine, and broth, you still get a delicious, creamy, almost pasta-like dish, with the nutty farro flavor. Try it both ways and see which you prefer... maybe the lighter rice risotto in the summer and a more robust farotto in the winter.

INGREDIENTS   *Makes 6-8 servings*

- 1 oz dry Porcini mushrooms (may sub 8 oz minced fresh cultivated mushrooms)
- 1 medium onion, 4-6 oz
- 1-1½ lb small mixed mushrooms
- 2 T (tablespoons) olive oil

- sea salt and fresh ground pepper
- 1½ cups Carnaroli risotto rice or 1½ cups Einkorn Farro
- ½ cup white wine, dry sherry, or marsala
- 6 cups seasoned broth (add 1 t salt if broth is unsalted)

- ½ cup freshly grated Parmesan cheese (2 oz) plus more to pass at serving if desired
- 2 T parsley
- 1 T each fresh sage, thyme and oregano (or 1 t each dried)

PREPARATION

- If using einkorn farro, I suggest soaking the grain 1-12 hours to reduce the 45+ minute cooking time.

- Rehydrate dry mushrooms by barely covering with water in a small saucepan. Bring to a boil, turn off heat, cover and let sit 20 minutes. Pull out the mushrooms, squeeze dry, and use like raw mushrooms. Use the liquid in the broth, but avoid any grit at the bottom.

- Bring broth to a simmer, cover and turn off heat.

- Small chop onions and finely chop the mushrooms.

- Heat oil in a 3 quart pan. Sauté onion and mushrooms on medium high. Once they begin to soften, salt and pepper to taste, lower heat to medium and cook 3 minutes more.

preparation continues next page . . .

■ Risotto

• Add Carnaroli rice and 10-16 grinds pepper. Stir to coat 1-2 minutes. Add wine, stirring as it boils off.

• **Traditional way**: Add hot broth 1 cup at a time. Adjust the heat so the risotto stays at a bubble. Stir often and let the liquid absorb (it will still be thick and creamy), before adding the next cup. It should take about 3 minutes for each addition. You should end up using about 5¼ cups of broth total.

• **Marianne's way**: Add 5¼ cups of hot broth right at the start, savingthe rest for later, if needed. Adjust the heat so the risotto is at a medium bubble. Stir from the bottom up every 2-3 minutes until liquid is absorbed and risotto is thick and creamy.

• Grate the cheese and chop the herbs.

• If the rice seems too hard after 22 minutes and 5 ¼ cups broth, add ¼ cup more broth, stir, turn down and cover for 2-3 minutes. This should do it.

• Repeat if needed. Once the rice is al dente (soft with a firm center), stir in herbs, cheese, plus salt and pepper if needed. Let sit 3-5 minutes.

• Pass extra cheese or drizzle with olive oil if desired.

■ Farrotto

• Add the einkorn farro and 10-16 grinds of pepper to the pot. Stir to coat grains with the oil. Add wine, stirring as it boils off. Note the time.

• Add 5¼ cups hot broth, leaving ¾ cup for use later. Cover and simmer 25 minutes, stirring thoroughly every 4-5 minutes.

• Uncover and adjust heat to maintain a medium bubble. Stir from the bottom up every 3-4 minutes.

• Grate the cheese and chop the herbs.

• If the farro doesn't seem cooked (soft with a firm center) after 40-45 minutes and there isn't much liquid, add ¼ cup more broth, stir, turn down and cover for 2-3 minutes. This should do it.

• Repeat if needed. Once the farro is cooked (soft, but still with a chewy "bite"), stir in herbs, cheese, plus salt and pepper if needed. Let sit 3-5 minutes.

Pass extra cheese or drizzle with olive oil if desired.

Peaches and Farro

This is a delicious, unusual, nutritious, and simple side dish that takes advantage of summer's bounty. It would go terrific with chicken or pork, or, of course, a vegetarian feast like the one in the photo to the left. We had an Indian Summer dinner of peaches with farro, garden cucumber salad in sour cream, and sautéed Romano beans from the garden.

INGREDIENTS

Makes about 9 cups

1 lb emmer farro

1½ t salt

2 T olive oil

2 ½ oz red onions

½-1 t salt

¼ t sugar

¼-½ t fresh ground pepper

2 lbs farmer fresh peaches (you could substitute nectarines)

¼+ t coriander; may sub garam masala, ginger or cinnamon

¼+ t cumin, optional

dash (or more) of cayenne

PREPARATION

• Prepare farro. This can be done up to two days ahead (see recipe at the beginning of this chapter).

• Peel, then sliver onions from stem end to root end, cutting so pieces are about 2" long and ¼" wide.

• Sauté the onions in a lidded pan in 1-2 T olive oil over medium or less heat. Start with the pan uncovered. Salt after 5 minutes. Add sugar and pepper after another 5 minutes.

• You could add a splat of port instead of sugar.

• Cover the pan and cook at a low heat 15-25 minutes until onions are totally "pooped". This can also be done ahead.

• When ready to assemble the dish, slice the peaches lengthwise into ⅛'s or thinner.

• Add onions back to sauté pan if you made them ahead. If liquid is needed, add a little oil or maybe white wine or port. Once they begin to warm, add the peaches and cook about 5 minutes until they start to soften. Add spices, stir and taste.

• Add the farro and cook another 5 minutes. Adjust seasonings.

Bumper nectarine crop from Marianne's tree

Butternut Blue Cheese Farrotto or Risotto

This comes out a lovely orange color and is wonderful as a vegetarian meal or a side to any autumn meal. Enjoy with a winter greens salad (escarole, frissee, endive, radicchio) and steamed broccoli or Brussels sprouts. This would also be a nice accompaniment to roasted or grilled meat.

Original watercolor by Bill McCarrol

INGREDIENTS

Makes 6-8+ servings

1 ¼ cups finely chopped onion

2 large garlic cloves minced

1½-2 lbs butternut squash

2 t chopped fresh rosemary, divided

6 cups broth, (+ 1 t salt if using unsalted broth)

2 T butter or good olive oil

1 ½ cups einkorn farro

¾ cup dry white wine

3 oz chopped baby spinach leaves, optional

½ cup freshly grated Parmesan cheese

½ cup crumbled blue cheese (2 ounces)

PREPARATION

- Chop onion and garlic, and peel and seed squash. Shred the squash with a food processor or mince it by hand. You will use 3-4 cups. Add the seeds and any extra flesh to the broth, or save if you have another use for it.

- Bring broth to a simmer, cover and turn off.

- Melt butter in a 3 qt. lidded sauté or 6 qt soup pot. Sauté onion & garlic on medium, about 5-8 minutes. Salt & pepper.

- Once onions soften, add squash and 1½ t rosemary; sauté 4-6 minutes to begin to soften it, stirring to coat with butter. Salt and pepper.

- Add einkorn and 10-16 grinds pepper. Stir to coat 1-2 minutes. Add wine, stirring as it absorbs and boils off. Note the time.

- Add 5 ¼ cups of the hot broth (strain out squash bits if you put them in). Cover and simmer 25 minutes, stirring thoroughly every 4-5 minutes.

- Uncover and adjust heat to maintain a medium bubble. Stir from the bottom up every 3-4 minutes.

- If the farro doesn't seem cooked after 40-45 minutes and there isn't much liquid, add ¼ cup more broth, stir, turn down and cover for 2-3 minutes. This should do it, but repeat if needed. Once it seems ready, turn off heat and let rest 3-5 minutes.

- Stir in spinach leaves and cheeses after the rice rests. If it is too thick, add a little broth. Sprinkle with remaining ½ t rosemary and serve.

Fig Risotto with Prosciutto

I really love figs and use them a lot in my cooking. They are sweet, tender, and filled with tiny crunchy seeds that give them an interesting texture, and provide lots of fiber. Their super sweet flavor is good in desserts, but also goes well in dishes with sharp or savory flavors. Fresh figs are very delicate and don't travel well, so many stores don't even carry them. Look for fresh figs in late summer and early fall and grab them when you can.

Einkorn is a bit "softer" than emmer farro and really takes well to the risotto style preparation. The amount of liquid needed is the same, it just takes longer to cook. Adding all the liquid at once works especially well with the einkorn.

INGREDIENTS

Makes 8-10 sides, or about 6 main dish servings

1 ½ lbs figs, green if possible but any will do

2 T extra virgin olive oil

2 t rosemary

¼ c minced prosciutto or pancetta

½ c chopped onion

1 ½ c short or medium grain rice

6 cups broth

½ c dry white wine

¼ c grated parmesan cheese

Parmesan curls to serve, optional

PREPARATION

• Heat broth to a boil. Cover and turn off heat.

• Select the 8 largest figs and cut in half. Cut the rest in ½" pieces.

• Heat 2 t oil and add figs, cut side down. Cook to sizzle and brown about 2 minutes. Turn cut side up and sprinkle with salt, pepper and rosemary. Set aside to garnish risotto at serving.

• Add the remaining oil to the pan. Saute the prosciutto and onion until golden. Salt (lightly!) and pepper as they cook.

• Add rice and stir 2 minutes. Add wine and stir until it absorbs.

• Add 5 ¼ cups broth all at once or add 1 cup at a time as it absorbs (3-5 minutes). Add 1 t salt if the broth is unsalted. Keep rice at a gentle bubble - a strong simmer. Stir every 2-3 minutes.

• After 12 minutes, add half the chopped figs.

• If, after 20 minutes, the liquid is gone and the rice does not seem done, add more broth ½ cup at a time. Stir gently.

• Once it seems close to done, add the rest of the chopped figs and the grated cheese. Turn off the heat and let the risotto sit partly covered for a few minutes.

• Reheat the halved figs and either put on the rice if serving as a buffet or put two on each plate along with the cheese curls.

COOK'S NOTES

• Use less salt than normal, as the prosciutto adds a fair bit of sodium. As you are cooking, if your dish doesn't seem to have enough salt, add only ¼ t at a time.

Spinach & White Bean Pesto Pasta

The "pesto" featured in this recipe is made with spinach and not basil, so it retains its brilliant green color even if reheated the next day in a microwave. The presentation with the vivid green, the red tomatoes and the white feta is stunning.

This dish is substantial enough on its own, or serve it with sautéed mushrooms and slivers of fennel and onion, or garlicky braised broccolini with red pepper flakes. It would also be great beside slices of grilled steak.

INGREDIENTS

Makes 4 servings & 2½ cups pesto

½ pound spinach (fresh or frozen)

2 c cooked white beans, divided

6-8 cloves garlic, peeled and chopped

2 T fresh lemon juice

3 T olive oil

⅓ t sea salt, or to taste

black or red pepper to taste (⅛ t +)

8 oz of good quality rustic pasta, maybe a farro pasta

4-6 oz crumbled feta cheese

2+ fresh tomatoes, about 1 lb, or 8 oz cherry tomatoes

   OR 4 oz rehydrated dried tomatoes

Olive oil to drizzle at serving, optional

MAKE THE PESTO

• Make the pesto 1-24 hours ahead - it only gets better!

• Steam and drain the spinach, if fresh. Thaw and drain, if frozen.

• Add the spinach, 1¼ cup of the beans, and the next five ingredients to a food processor or blender. Puree until smooth and adjust seasonings. It should have a nice bite!

PUTTING IT TOGETHER

• Boil water in a 4 quart pot with 2½ t salt.

• Cook pasta until al dente, 12-16 minutes at a boil.

• Meanwhile, crumble the feta and small dice the tomatoes or quarter the cherry tomatoes. Toss the tomatoes with a bit of salt, pepper, olive oil and a dash of sugar.

• Drain the pasta, leaving just enough water to keep it moist or drizzle in some good olive oil.

• Put pasta into bowls or onto pre-warmed plates. Top with the pesto, feta, tomatoes and remaining beans. Enjoy!

USING UP ANY EXTRA PESTO

• The pesto is also great on and in soups and stews, either dolloped on top or as a base for a minestrone type soup.

• Enjoy it on pita chips, or as a dip for crudité.

• Try it tossed with freshly steamed cauliflower.

Pear Pasta with Prosciutto, Peas and Pecorino

We've enjoyed this dish alongside shoulder lamb chops, but it would go well with any meat. Or, leave out the ham and do a trio of vegetable dishes.

This is the perfect type of recipe that might benefit from a light drizzle of a thick balsamic vinegar at serving time. This is especially true if you are having it for leftovers and it needs a little "perk". Keep this tip in mind for any pasta dish that uses an oil or cream sauce.

PREPARATION

- Take the peas out of the freezer to thaw.

- Bring a large lidded pot (4-6 quart) of water to a boil.

- Quarter the pears lengthwise and core them. Slice them thinly crosswise.

- Melt half the butter in a large skillet and add all the smaller pear pieces when the butter begins sizzling. Let them sit a few minutes to color the bottom side. Salt and pepper them and shake the skillet to flip them or use a spatula. Cook a few more minutes. Pile them on a plate/tray that will hold all the pears, shallots and prosciutto.

- Cook the larger pieces of pear the same way, with more butter if needed plus salt and pepper. Put them in a separate pile from the smaller pieces.

- Slice or tear the prosciutto into small pieces (½ x 1 or 2"). Thinly slice the shallot top to bottom; you want about ⅔ cup. Chop the parsley. Once the pears are cooked, fry the prosciutto bits and shallots 4-6 minutes to crisp. Add to the tray in another pile.

- When the water comes to a boil, salt it (1+t) and again bring to a rolling boil. Add the pasta and stir a couple of times. Start timing according to the package directions when the water boils again. Keep it at a good boil, partly covered is fine.

- When the pasta is almost cooked, carefully pull out ½ cup of the cooking water and set aside.

- Drain the pasta when it is to your liking and put it into the skillet if it will fit, or back into the pot. Turn the heat to low.

- Add the crème fraiche and pecorino. Stir gently to coat the pasta.

- Add all the small pears, ⅔ of the peas, ⅔ of the prosciutto onion mix and ⅔ of the parsley. Taste and season with sea salt and fresh ground pepper as needed. If it seems dry, add some of the pasta water or more crème fraiche.

- Plate the pasta or put in a large serving bowl. Top with the remaining pears, peas, prosciutto and parsley.

INGREDIENTS

Makes 6 side servings

4 oz frozen baby peas

8 ounces pasta, farfalle or tagliatelle are nice

3 T unsalted butter

4 large pears

Salt and freshly ground pepper

2-3 large shallots or a small red onion, 4 oz

2 oz thin sliced prosciutto ham

½ cup crème fraiche (may sub sour cream but it is a stronger flavor)

½ c fresh grated Pecorino Romano or parmesan

2 T finely chopped flat-leaf parsley

Purple Pasta with Cabbage, Chevre, Walnut & Apple

This is unusual, eye-catching, quickly made and delicious! Enjoy it as a vegetarian dinner or serve with a side of lamb, pork, duck or chicken.

INGREDIENTS

Makes 8+ side servings, 4-5 as a main course

1 cup raw walnut pieces

1½ lb red cabbage

8 oz red onion

1 large or 2 medium crisp apples

3-4 T balsamic vinegar - more as needed for zing

2-3 T olive oil

4 oz chevre cheese

2 T fresh parsley

8 oz chunky pasta

sea salt and fresh ground pepper to taste

PREPARATION

- Bring 2½ quarts water to boil in a 3 quart pot. Add 1 t salt. (Save a bigger pot for the cabbage).
- Toast walnuts gently in a bit of olive oil. Chop into pieces if large.
- Cut onion into 1/4 or 1/6 wedges and thinly slice.
- Cut cabbage into 1/6 or 1/8 wedges. Discard core and thinly slice the rest.
- Cut apple into 1/6 wedges and core. Thinly slice.
- Once all veggies are chopped and water is boiling, add pasta and stir as it comes again to a boil. Adjust heat to maintain a gentle boil. Set timer from time of reboil according to package directions.
- Once pasta is cooking, mix vinegar and oil in a 4+ quart sauté or soup pan and heat.
- Add onion and cook 2 minutes.
- Add cabbage and cook 3-5 minutes, stirring to mix from bottom to top. Salt and pepper. Monitor heat, so it is making noise but not burning.
- Add apple once cabbage is almost wilted.
- Chop parsley and chevre.
- Once pasta is cooked, use a cup measure to take out ¾ cup water. Set aside.
- Drain the pasta and transfer it to the cabbage. Add the reserved cooking water as needed.
- Gently mix well. Taste and season as needed.
- As soon as it looks fantastic, turn off heat. Stir in the walnuts, ¾ of the cheese, ¾ of the parsley.
- Serve onto plates and top with remaining cheese and parsley.
- If desired, drizzle with a little specialty fig or plain balsamic vinegar at serving.
- Like so many other dishes, this is even better the next day!

Balsamic Braised Cabbage & Apples with Barley

This dish is essentially the "Purple Pasta" recipe without the pasta, cheese and nuts, and enhanced with cooked barley. Enjoy as a substantial grain side dish, a wonderful offering on a buffet, or even as an enlightened replacement for stuffing.

COOK'S NOTES

- This recipe will take longer (almost double the time) if ingredients are doubled. Use a 6 quart soup pot if recipe is increased.

- Savoy Cabbage takes less time to cook than regular green (or red) cabbage.

- If the dish needs to wait, undercook it a little and keep covered until ready to serve. It will keep cooking. Adjust seasonings to taste.

MODIFICATIONS

- Use 5-6 T apple cider vinegar in place of the Balsamic, and add 2 T mustard seeds and a bay leaf.

- Use 1-3 T currant jelly instead of sugar.

- Toast 1 t coriander seeds, grind them and add to the dish.

INGREDIENTS   *Makes about 5 cups, 6-10 servings*

2 cups cooked barley

8 oz red onion

1½ lb red, green or Savoy cabbage

2-4 T rich balsamic vinegar - more as needed for zing

2-3 T olive oil

2 -5 T water, broth, apple juice or cider

1 t sugar, if vinegar is not sweet

½ t sea salt

¼ -½ t fresh ground pepper

1 large or 2 medium crisp apples

PREPARATION

- Quarter onion top to bottom (peel first) and thinly slice crosswise. Do the same with the cabbage. Cut the cabbage quarters one more time top to bottom if they are really wide before thinly slicing.

- Mix vinegar and oil in a 10-12" sauté pan and heat to medium.

- Add onion and cook 1 minute.

- Add cabbage, 3 T liquid, sugar, salt and pepper. Mix all, cover, turn down a bit and cook 4-6 minutes, stirring occasionally until cabbage is soft and almost to taste. Monitor heat, so it is making noise but not burning. Add more liquid as needed.

- Cut the apples while the cabbage is cooking (no need to peel). Core them once they are quartered, and slice.

- Add apple and barley to cooked cabbage. Uncover and cook until mixture is softened to your taste, 2-4 minutes.

IF THE OVEN IS ON OR THE STOVE IS FULL, MAKE THIS VERSION

- Use same ingredients as above except ½ cup liquid.

- Preheat oven to 425.

- Use a lidded oven proof pan.

- Sauté onions as above. Add everything except apples. Mix, cover and bake 20 minutes. Mix in apples, cover and cook another 10 minutes.

- If there is a lot of liquid, leave uncovered. Check after five minutes and cover if all liquid is gone.

Barbecue Heirloom Beans

This is not sweet, like traditional baked beans, but savory, like salsa. These go great with any kind of grilled or roasted meat, or with a good tamale, or served alongside polenta. Seasoning options are infinite. Go with the recipe below or feel free to improvise. As long as every ingredient is delicious and full of flavor, the final product will be too!

PREPARATION

• Follow package directions for soaking and cooking beans. Add 3 garlic cloves and the bay leaf. Cook times are on the package. Beans can be cooked up to 2 days ahead.

• To test beans, scoop out a few in a spoon and blow on them. If the skins peel open, they're done. Once cooked, season with ½+ t sea salt, a splash of olive oil and red pepper to taste.

• Beans can be cooled in their liquid and stored refrigerated 2-4 days. If the liquid is thin, pour most of it off and boil it down.

PREPARE THE OPTION A ADD-INS

• Mince and sauté the onions and peppers in olive oil until soft and as crispy as you like. Salt (½+ t) and pepper to taste as they cook. Add the rest in the last couple of minutes. Turn off heat when done.

COOK'S NOTES

If you have some leftover, turn it into a **Bean Dip**:

• Mash or puree some or all of the leftovers. Put in an ovenproof dish and cover with shredded jack or quark cheese.

• Bake at 250-350 for 15-25 minutes until bubbly.

• Serve with warmed corn tortillas or tortilla chips.

FINAL ASSEMBLY

• Drain the cooked beans, but don't discard the liquid. Add the Option A or B add-ins to the beans and 1½ cups of the cooking liquid, still saving the rest. Simmer low 10-30 minutes; stir occasionally to meld flavors. Add back cooking liquid as needed.

• The beans will thicken and the flavor will deepen by the next day, so save the cooking liquid to add when needed.

• Top with chopped herbs at serving, if desired.

INGREDIENTS

Makes about 3-4 cups, 5-8 servings

½ lb (½ the bag) dry Borlotti, Rio Zape or Good Mother Stallard beans

6 cloves garlic, divided 3 & 3

1 bay leaf

½ t+ sea salt, fresh ground and hot pepper to taste

1 t Spanish Pimenton de la Vera (smoked paprika)

hot pepper to taste

chopped fresh cilantro or scallions, at serving

ADD-IN OPTION A
(need to sauté)

3-4½ cups total, minced onion, mildly spicy anaheim or poblano-type pepper, roasted or fresh tomatoes

2 T flavorful olive oil

3 cloves minced garlic (from above)

ADD-IN OPTION B
(no cook)

1 cup prepared salsa (the best you can find!) or ½+ cup Barbecue or Enchilada Sauce

3 cloves minced garlic (from above)

2 T flavorful olive oil

Jerry Mon's Red Beans and Rice

*R*ed *Beans and Rice are a classic Louisiana Creole dish. It is traditionally served on Monday's and uses the ham bone and meat scraps left over from Sunday supper. I hadn't made it in years, but I had some locally grown medium sized red beans to sample, so there I was. In this photo, it is served with sausage.*

INGREDIENTS

Makes about 3 quarts, 8 main or 18 side servings

1 lb red beans, soaked 48 hours in 2 quarts water

1½ lbs meaty ham shank, cracked in pieces

1½-2 quarts fresh water / stock

1 T oil or butter

2 onions

1 green pepper, optional

1 c celery

4 cloves garlic

paprika

white, red, black pepper

3 bay leaves

Thyme/savory/oregano

- tie fresh stems to make a bouquet garni or add 2 t dried total

2 T Worcestershire

2 fresh small chopped tomatoes or 1 can roasted diced tomatoes, optional

3+ t salt, to taste

3 cups raw rice or dry polenta

1 bunch scallions, green and white parts thinly sliced, at serving, optional

PREPARATION

- Bring first 3 ingredients to a simmer and skim off any scum.

- Sauté the vegetables in oil or butter for 5-8 minutes until they start to soften. Do NOT salt.

- Stir in spices and cook 5 minutes more. Add this to the beans once the scum has stopped forming on the top.

- Partly cover the beans and simmer gently until they are tender 45 -90 minutes.

- Once beans are cooked, pull out the ham shank and let it cool. Pull out the bouquet garni (herb sprigs) and discard them. Add worcestershire and tomatoes and simmer 15 minutes uncovered.

- Pull any meat off the shanks once cool. Chop and add back to the pot.

- Taste and salt as desired, but less is more. Try ½ t at first.

- The beans can be cooked to this point and let cool and refrigerated for use the next day. Gently reheat, taste and adjust seasonings.

- Cook rice or polenta when ready to serve the beans.

- Top with chopped scallions at serving if desired.

* recipe inspired by my dear friend, Jerry McGinley

COOK'S NOTES

- Red beans are NOT the same as kidney beans. They are about half the size. One could substitute a small pink bean.

- If possible, make the beans 1-2 days ahead, as the flavors meld and deepen with time.

- Serve over rice . . . or break with tradition and use polenta.

- Try serving as a side dish with BBQ shrimp, marinated grilled chuck steak or London broil, collard greens, and/or sweet potato salad.

Carib Rice & Red Lentils

This is a deliciously aromatic, full-protein dish with a bit of warmth. If you're making it for a party, the ingredients can double or triple easily.

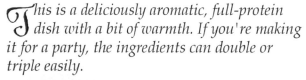

Red lentils may be tiny compared to other legumes, but they are big in nutrition. They are a terrific source of fiber in your diet (both soluble and insoluble) and are associated with the ability to lower cholesterol and reduce the risk of coronary artery disease. Red lentils are also high in the mineral molybdenum that can help detoxify your body.

INGREDIENTS

Makes 2 quarts,
6-8 side servings

1 ¼ cups of a medium grain, paella-type rice (Spanish, if possible)

½ cup red lentils

⅛ t celery seed

1 ½ t sea salt

⅛ t chili powder

¼ t paprika

½ t coriander (+ more to taste)

½ cup small chop (canned) hatch chiles OR

  1 minced jalapeno OR

   ½ cup minced roasted red peppers

¾ cup minced onion

½ stalk (edible part only) minced lemongrass (optional)

1-2 cups coconut milk (light or regular)

Broth or water to make 3 cups liquid total

PREPARATION

- Combine spices in a small bowl and mix well.

- Combine rice, red lentils, onions and peppers in a large bowl. Add the spices and stir well.

- Add coconut milk and other liquid and mix well.

- Grease a 2 quart baking dish and transfer the rice mixture to it.

- Cover with foil and bake at 350 for 30 minutes. (confirm time!)Let rest covered 30 minutes.

- Serve now, hold for an hour or so or uncover to cool. Reheat covered in the oven about 20-30 minutes at 350.

- May need to add ½ cup or so liquid on the reheat if it seems dry.

THAI STYLE OPTION

- Replace the chili powder, paprika and chiles/jalapeno with 1 t (or more) Thai red curry paste.

127

Marianne's Garden

◀ *The Chef at work in her garden*

Marianne tilling the garden soil ▲

Rays of sunshine in Marianne's garden haven ▲

▲ *A good days harvest from Marianne's summer vegetable garden* ▶

Entrées

Black Bean, Butternut Squash & Sausage Stew

This stew offers a rich spicy profile via an apple cider reduction, allspice berries, and Worcestershire sauce. It is delicious as a stew or could be made thicker and served over rice as a side dish. For vegetarians, simply leave out the sausage.

INGREDIENTS

Makes 5-6 quarts

1 lb dry black beans; about 2 cups

5 garlic cloves, peeled

1 t allspice berries

2 bay leaves

1 dried red chile, optional

1 lb spicy smoked sausage

2 medium or 1 huge onion (10-12 oz)

1-3 T olive oil for sauté

4 cups apple cider or juice

4 cups broth, un- or lightly salted, preferably homemade

2½ lb butternut squash, or sweet potatoes

2 cups tomato, seeded & chopped; canned is fine

salt & pepper

3-4 T ketchup

2 t Worcestershire sauce

½-1 t allspice

hot sauce to taste

chopped green onions at serving

dollop of sour cream

PREPARATION

• Soak beans overnight in a cool place. Do not drain.

• Transfer to a 3 quart pot and add water if needed to cover by 2 inches.

• Bring to a boil and skim off foam with a small metal colander or large slotted spoon.

• Put allspice berries in infuser or tie up in cheese cloth. Add this, bay leaves, garlic cloves, and pepper to beans.

• Simmer gently, partly covered until tender (1-2 hours). Marianne's Black Valentine Heirloom Beans may take 2+ hours.

• Seed & peel squash. Cut into ½ - ¾" cubes.

• If desired, remove sausage casing. Quarter links and cut into ½" chunks. Chop the onion into ½" pieces - pinky to thumbnail size.

• Sauté sausage in a soup pot. Add olive oil if needed. Try to let it get quite hot and browned, but not smoking and burned. Turn off the heat and use a large slotted spoon or other tool to remove.

• Turn the heat back on to medium-high and add the onion. Add oil only if needed. After 3-5 minutes, season with sea salt and pepper.

• Once onions soften and begin to color, add the cider. Bring to a brisk boil and boil down to half. Add 4 cups broth and bring to a boil.

• Add tomatoes and squash. Bring to a simmer and maintain until squash just softens, 10-15 minutes.

• Add the cooked beans and 1-2 cups of their water - save the rest to thin the stew later as desired. Add seasonings and simmer partly covered, about 10 minutes.

• Add the sausage and simmer 10 minutes. Taste and adjust seasonings.

• Pulse a few times in an immersion blender to thicken the soup, or add bean water to thin it as needed. It will thicken as it sits, especially by the next day.

• At serving, garnish with chopped green onions and/or sour cream, and pass the hot sauce.

COOK'S NOTES

• Use a tea infuser ball or cheese cloth for the spices in the beans.

• Canned beans may be used in a pinch. You'll need 3-4 cans. Drain well and increase seasoning.

• The squash can be par cooked if preferred.

• Sweet potatoes or other winter squash can stand in for the butternut.

Marianne's Fasolakia Yiahni (Greek Stew)

This main course variation on the Greek dish of the same name uses three summer vegetables and has the sunny seasonings of lemon and feta cheese. Serve it in big bowls with crusty bread and a simple lettuce salad with a bold dressing.

INGREDIENTS

Makes 5 quarts;
Serves 9-12 as main dish

3-5 T olive oil

2 huge onions (about 1 ½ lbs)

3 garlic cloves

salt & pepper

3 lbs ripe tomatoes

¾ cup parsley

3 lbs boiling potatoes

½ cup white wine

2½ pounds fresh green beans

½ lb feta cheese

2 lbs (or more) popcorn shrimp or chunks of white fish, optional

⅓+ cup fresh lemon juice (1-2 lemons)

Crusty bread at serving

PREPARATION

• Chop the vegetables as you go along.

• Medium chop the onions and mince the garlic. Sauté the onion in the olive oil on medium high in a 6 quart soup pot that has a lid. Season and add the garlic after a few minutes and continue until onions start to color (6-9 min total).

• Use a lid if it gets too dry.

• Small chop the tomatoes and the parsley.

• Lower heat to medium. Add tomatoes and half the parsley and cover. Cook 5-7 minutes until tomatoes begin to mush.

• Meanwhile chunk the potatoes (unpealed) and salt and pepper them on the cutting board.

• Push the tomato mixture to one side and add half the potatoes. Push the tomatoes the other way, and put in the rest of the potatoes. Move the tomatoes back across the top. Having someone hold the pan at an angle helps. Pour white wine on top.

• Cover, stabilize at a low boil and cook 10 minutes or until potatoes just begin to soften. String the beans and slice to about 1½" long.

• Stir in beans. Salt and pepper if needed.

• Cover and raise heat to make a low boil. Cook until the beans start to soften, 8-12 minutes.

• The stew can be cooked ahead up to this point.

• To continue, bring stew to a low boil and cook until the beans are just cooked to your taste.

• Toss in the frozen shrimp or fish chunks, and give them 2-3 minutes to begin to color. Toast the bread now, too.

• Once the shrimp are hot, turn off heat. Crumble the feta. Add it, the lemon juice and the parsley. Adjust seasonings to taste.

• Stir gently and let rest two minutes.

COOK'S NOTES

• Prep time for this dish is 30-45 minutes plus 15-20 more to stew.

• There really isn't time to do anything else while making this unless you chop ahead.

• You will need a 6-8 quart soup pot with lid, and a citrus juicer.

Chilean Bean & Corn Stew

This dish, Porotos Granados, is Chile's national bean dish - and rightfully so. It is delicious and rib-sticking. The flavors combine so wonderfully, each complementing and building on the other, to offer up something truly bigger than the sum of its parts! Dry or fresh Borlotti beans, sometimes called "cranberry beans", are wonderful in this recipe.

PREP BEANS

- Soak dry beans overnight in 6+ cups water. Drain water and put beans in a 3+ quart pot with bay leaves and water to cover by 2-3". Partly cover the pan and gently boil 45 minutes to 2 hours until soft to the bite. Fresh beans (shuck before cooking) will take 10-15 minutes.

- Once cooked, salt and pepper to taste. Save liquid to use as broth.

PREP SQUASH AND CORN

Squash needs to be cubed and par boiled. Here are two options:

- Peel and chop raw. To do this, cut the round end off and peel the top and bottom separately. Then small chunk it. Par boil covered 5-8 minutes in 1" boiling, lightly salted and sugared water, until just soft. Save water for corn and stew.

- OR halve the squash, seed and par-roast at 375 for 30-50 minutes until softened, but not mushy. Once cool, skin and chop the flesh into small chunks.

- Shuck and par boil corn 4 minutes in a 6+ quart pot with ½" of lightly salted and sugared water. Remove from water and cover with damp towel to cool. Measure and save cooking water for stew.

- When cool, cut corn off cobs. You'll puree ⅔ of this.

COMBINE STEW

- Bring 8 cups of the vegetable waters / broth to a boil in a big pot. Enhance with bouillon base or salt & pepper as needed.

- Small chop the onion, grate the carrot and add to the boiling broth. Stir gently. Simmer 8 minutes.

- Puree ⅔ of the corn, using wine to thin. Add all the corn to the stew, along with the beans and squash. Salt and pepper to taste and stir gently. Simmer 15-30 minutes, stirring every few minutes.

- Season to taste after 20 minutes.

- Add extra broth as needed. The stew usually thickens if made ahead.

MAKE PAPRIKA OIL

- Mince garlic. Gently heat garlic and oil.

- Once garlic begins to color, turn heat off and add paprika. Careful, it is easy to burn!

INGREDIENTS

Makes about 5-6 quarts

1 lb Borlotti beans, soaked overnight or 4 lbs fresh in the shell - to make 6 cups shelled

2 bay leaves

2 ½-3 lbs butternut squash

9 ears corn, to make 5-6 cups shucked, about 2 lbs

OR 2 lbs frozen corn

8-10 cups broth, preferably homemade from this recipe

1 huge onion, about 14-16 oz

2 large carrots, about 4-6 oz

¾ c dry white wine

1 ½ + t sea salt, ½+ t fresh ground pepper

½ cup walnut oil, or soy/olive mix

5 cloves garlic, crushed

4 t paprika

25 basil leaves

AT SERVING

- Just before serving, stack basil leaves and thinly slice them crosswise (chiffonade). Don't chop ahead as it turns black.

- Stir paprika oil. Drizzle on stew and scatter the basil artfully.

- Stir any remaining garnishes into the pot of stew.

Cauliflower & Pasta with Currants and Pignoli

This is a wonderful main course, or serve with braised artichokes, a fennel salad and a piece of grilled meat. Southern Italians cook cauliflower like this but not with the added pasta.

INGREDIENTS

Makes 4-6 main servings,
8+ as a side

½ c dried currants (or raisins)

⅓ c white wine

½ c pignoli (pine nuts)

1 large head cauliflower

2-4 T extra virgin olive oil

6 anchovy fillets

10 oz orecchiette, campanele or
   other short pasta

½-¾ t red pepper flakes

1 T butter or olive oil

½ c fresh bread crumbs

2-3 oz Pecorino or sharp
   parmesan cheese, grated

PREPARATION

• Salt and heat water to a boil in 6 quart pot.

• Combine currants and wine and either microwave 20 seconds or warm on stove to plump up the currants.

• Chop cauliflower into 1 inch pieces.

• When water boils, blanch cauliflower just 5 minutes total (it will cook more while sauteeing later). Transfer cauliflower to a colander with a slotted spoon. Drain 1 minute.

• Heat oil in very large sauté pan. Mash anchovies and sauté them. Turn this off for a minute or 2 before adding cauliflower.

• Carefully add cauliflower to anchovy oil, turn heat back on and toss florets to glaze and cook.

• In a medium sauté pan, toast pine nuts 2-3 minutes on medium. You'll reuse the pan for the bread crumbs.

• Add pasta to boiling water that was used to cook cauliflower. Set timer according to package directions.

• Heat butter in pine nut sauté pan and add bread crumbs. Stir and cook on low 3-5 minutes to color.

• Once cauliflower starts to color, add red pepper flakes, turn up heat and pour in currants and their liquid. Boil this off. Add pine nuts and turn heat to medium low.

• Grate ⅔ of cheese into a bowl (use rest at serving).

• When pasta is al dente, scoop out a cup of cooking water with a coffee mug. Drain the rest of the pasta.

• Gently mix cauliflower, pasta, ½ cup of the reserved water, and cheese. Add more red pepper to taste

• Sprinkle on bread crumbs and grate a little extra cheese on each plate as you serve.

Mulligatawny Stew

This rich, hearty soup, with a golden hue, has wonderful Indian spices and was a favorite of the British when they ruled India. I have seen versions of this stew that are thin like a soup. This one is thick and rib-sticking. A bowl of this over rice is a satisfying meal.

Mulligatawny is traditionally made with red lentils. I have modified this recipe to also use heirloom tepary beans, which have more protein than most legumes. They do not break down like lentils and have a heavenly aroma when cooking.

INGREDIENTS

Makes 7-8 quarts - 20 servings over rice

1 whole chicken, poached and shredded (about 2 lbs seasoned meat) OR use a skinned and shredded rotisserie chicken

4 quarts flavorful stock - from poaching (see recipe for Meat Stocks in "Savory Soups" chapter). A store bought mix of low sodium chicken and vegetable broths may be substituted.

1-5 T olive oil

2½ large onions, small chop, about 24 oz

6 celery ribs, finely chopped (2-2½ cups)

10 cloves garlic, minced

4 T fresh ginger, finely grated or minced

2 T Madras curry powder

1 T ground cumin

2 t ground coriander

1½ t dry thyme or 1½ T fresh leaves (no stems)

1 t cayenne - add ½ t more or less at end to taste

1 t black pepper

1 t sea salt - add more if broth is unsalted

1½ lbs red lentils or brown tepary beans

1¼ lbs carrots, small dice

1½ lbs small (non-russet) potatoes, small dice OR use part or all sweet potato

5 granny smith apples, about 6-8 cups chopped

5 T fresh lemon juice

1 lb frozen peas or spinach or mix

GARNISH INGREDIENTS

1 c shredded toasted coconut

plain yogurt

OPTIONAL CONDIMENTS

naan or other nice bread, plain or toasted, topped with chutney and cheddar cheese

mango cilantro relish salad

preparation on next page . . .

PREPARATION

- I recommend poaching the chicken in the morning or the night before. Then shred the chicken before you start the recipe, whether you poached it yourself or purchased a rotisserie chicken.

- Store shredded chicken just covered in your stock/broth. Taste the stock and adjust seasoning so it is flavorful but not too salty.

- If using tepary beans, soak overnight in 9 cups of water. Then, simmer them in a 3 quart pot (covered) with 2 cloves garlic and a bay leaf for 50-75 minutes until tender. Add boiling water as needed to keep beans immersed by 1". If using red lentils, they will be added to the dish later in the recipe.

- Make stock, poach, and shred chicken ahead. Store shredded chicken just covered in broth. Taste the stock and adjust seasoning so it is flavorful but not too salty.

- Use an 8+ quart pot for making the soup.

- Heat the olive oil and sauté onion on medium-high. As it softens, add the celery and season with salt and pepper.

- Once the celery begins to soften, turn heat to medium and add the garlic and ginger. Cook 3 minutes.

- Add the spices and cook another minute.

- Chop carrots and potatoes and add, along with 3 quarts of the stock. Cover and bring to a gentle boil. Cook for 12-25 minutes until vegetables are just soft.

- After 10 minutes, add cooked tepary beans or raw lentils. Keep at a very gentle boil.

- Meanwhile core and small dice or chop the apples. Toss them with the lemon juice to keep them from browning.

- Once the beans or lentils have softened (15-20 minutes), add the apples and chicken, and cook 20-30 minutes. Lower the heat so it doesn't boil, just have it steam.

- Spread the coconut on a parchment-lined tray and put into a cold oven set to 250. Toast for about 8 minutes, until golden, but check often (every few minutes after the first 5 minutes) because it browns quickly.

- Once the apples are at a consistency you like, add the peas.

- Turn off heat and let rest at least 10 minutes.

- Taste and adjust seasonings. Mulligatawny should have a bite but not be lethal.

- Serve topped with the coconut and a dollop of yogurt. This rich soup with a golden hue has wonderful Indian spices. The red lentils offer body, color, fiber, and a healthy protein-carb combination.

- The chicken can be omitted for vegetarians.

- Soup will thicken the next day - plan to thin to taste.

COOK'S NOTES

The name "Mulligatawny" comes from the Tamil words "mullaga" and "thanni" meaning "pepper-water". The dish is said to have been developed by Tamil Indian cooks to satisfy the tastes of the British stationed in India during the late 18th century.

There are endless variations to this recipe. Some use lamb instead of chicken, some add peanuts, coconut milk, tomatoes, etc.

Despite the long list of ingredients, it is not very difficult to make. Experiment and enjoy!

Thai Green Curry Stew

This is REALLY delicious! It is a simple recipe, as long as you have a small food processor for making the paste. The vegetable ingredients are not hard and fast; use what you can get that looks the freshest and most flavorful, or have on hand. You will need about 1 lb of meat or fish and 4 lbs of vegetables. Everything comes together quickly, as you chop and cook. In about an hour, you'll be eating and wondering how you got to Thailand so quickly!

INGREDIENTS

Makes 3+ quarts - serves 8 as a main dish

GREEN CURRY BASE

¼ c water

10 jalapeños, seeds optional

12 cloves garlic

3 T mint & cilantro stems (save leaves for serving)

1½ T ginger, peeled and coarse chop

3 stalks lemongrass

⅔ t salt

3 T vegetable oil

3 T minced shallot or red onion

1 T coriander

1 t cumin

3 T lime zest (2+ limes)

THE CONTENTS

1 lb shrimp

6 oz onion

6 oz red, yellow, orange peppers

8 oz eggplant

8 oz mushrooms

6 oz green beans (carrots, potatoes, etc…)

16 oz garden zucchini

6 oz garden chard, stalks chopped with onions

olive, coconut or other oil for sauté

preparation on following page . . .

THE REST OF THE CURRY SAUCE

2 t fish sauce

1 T brown sugar

2¼ cans or 19 oz coconut milk

2-3 cups broth + the vegetable cooking water

AT SERVING

½ c chopped basil

½ c chopped cilantro

½ c chopped mint

8-16 oz tomato, small chop, optional

5 oz mung bean sprouts, optional

THE RICE

2 c brown rice

1½ t salt, or to taste

COOK'S NOTES

• I have yet to visit Thailand, so I say with abandon that this can be made with beef or chicken and the vegetables can be varied, too. Just think about how each ingredient will be best cooked and proceed accordingly.

• I put 2-3 times the vegetables in everything I make, and that is reflected in this recipe. Modify as desired.

PREPARATION

- Start rice first, 60 minutes before you plan to serve.
- Cook as you normally do, or try the method below.

ONE WAY TO MAKE BROWN RICE

- Rinse rice in a strainer under cold running water for 30 seconds. For 2 cups rice, bring 7-8 cups of salted water to a boil in a heavy pot with a tight-fitting lid. Add the rice, stir it once, and bring it again to a boil. Boil it partly covered or uncovered, for 30 minutes.
- Drain the rice and save the water for soup. Let it drain 10 seconds, then return it to the pot. Cover and let it steam for 10 to 30 minutes just with its own heat (burner turned off). Uncover, fluff with a fork, and season with salt as desired.

PREPARING THE CURRY

- Make the curry base by combining ingredients in a food processor. Process to a paste, stopping 3 or 4 times to scrape down the sides.
- If using, chop fish into large bite size chunks. Peel shrimp and chop if desired. Set aside in a cool place.
- Chop vegetables into desired sizes. This is totally personal preference, but worth thinking about. I like to do slivers of onion and pepper, thin sliced mushrooms and eggplant, short pieces of beans, small chunks of zucchini, and ribbons of chard.
- In a 6 quart pot, sauté the onions, chard stems and peppers in a little oil at medium high heat. Season with salt and pepper to taste and transfer to a bowl. Sauté the mushrooms and eggplant this same way. Use the lid if the saute seems to get dry. If you plan to use the same pan to cook the curry, clean it. This will help to preserve the curry's bright green color.
- Par-cook the zucchini, beans, carrots, and potatoes in a lidded sauté pan with ¾" of boiling salted water, one vegetable at a time, to just soften (2-5 minutes each). Transfer each of the barely cooked vegetables to a colander, before adding the next one to the hot water. Finally, poach the fish (if using) in the same water. Gently simmer for 3-4 minutes. Save this water for the curry.
- When the vegetables are almost all par-cooked, add the curry paste to the 6 qt pot. Cook for 2-3 minutes, stirring often as it bubbles. Then add the fish sauce, brown sugar, and coconut milk, and simmer for 3 minutes.

- Chop the herbs and the tomato. Rinse the bean sprouts.
- Add the shrimp if using and simmer 2 minutes.
- Add cooked vegetables back in and 2½ cups broth. Return just to a boil, stir in half of the herbs and serve.

TO SERVE

- Serve in large wide bowls with rice.
- Garnish with about ¼ cup bean sprouts, a sprinkling of tomatoes, and 1 T of each herb per serving.
- Add any extra tomatoes and herbs to any remaining curry.

FREEZING INFORMATION

- Freeze extra curry in labeled 16 or 32 ounce deli containers for easy quick meals. I find that using like-shaped containers makes it easier to organize the freezer.
- To reheat the frozen curry, put in a pot on the stove or put in bowls to microwave.
- Freeze extra rice/farro in sandwich baggies in 4 oz portions. Push it to make a "tube", fold the top over and run a piece of masking tape around the middle of the tube (like the ring on a cigar, but mid-way along it).
- To reheat the frozen grain, put in a bowl and microwave for about 45 seconds, or warm in a double boiler on the stove-top.

Christmas Limas with Crispy Onions and Blue Cheese

I've served this dish as dinner over farro, and also over farro pasta with a green vegetable on the side. Every single bite is sublime. Christmas Limas keep their vivid markings even when cooked. They look like colorful skimming stones - and are nearly 2" long! This recipe could be a thoroughly decadent accompaniment to grilled or roasted meat.

INGREDIENTS

Makes about 4 cups

8 oz raw Christmas limas

1 lb red onions (about 2-3 medium)

2-3 T Blood Orange Olive Oil or other good quality fruity extra virgin olive oil

1½ T sea salt and pepper

4 oz blue cheese

3 T heavy cream, creme fraiche or half and half

⅓ cup bean cooking liquid, or as needed

PREPARATION

• Cull and rinse beans. Soak refrigerated in 4 cups water 8 hours or overnight.

• Cook beans covered at a simmer in about 6 cups water for 60-90 minutes. If desired, add a clove of garlic to the water.

• Once beans are cooked to your liking, add about ½ t salt to the water. Let beans cool.

• If you need to add more cooking water, heat it to a boil before adding it.

• Thinly slice the onions. Sauté over high heat in the olive oil. Salt and pepper once they begin to soften. Cook them on high so some get a bit blackened.

• Both steps can be done ahead of time.

• Combine the beans and the onions. Add the cheese, cream and bring to a simmer. Add bean cooking liquid, as needed, and season to taste.

Fig Balsamic Carnitas

I first served this made with pork at the Delicato Winery's 2012 Holiday Open House. We paired it to go with the Pinot Grigio in their new Sequin line. I also made it post-Thanksgiving 2013 and used roasted turkey legs for a tasting at Fine Wines of Stockton. Both were hits!

INGREDIENTS

**Fills about 40 small tortillas
or tops about 80 tortilla chips**

¾ c water

3 lbs pork shoulder, chopped into 1-2" pieces, or rotisserie chicken or cooked turkey legs

10 oz onion, finely chopped (more below)

½ t salt

¼ t medium red pepper flakes

3-4 T olive oil as needed

ADD TO COOKED PORK

1 ½ - 2 large onions (16 oz total) in 1" slivers

2 T good quality olive oil

½ t salt

1 bottle fruity white wine

¾ - 1 c good quality Fig Balsamic vinegar

PREPARATION

• Pour the water into a 4-5 quart Dutch oven or other heavy-lidded pan. Chop and add the pork shoulder and the first onion. Sprinkle with ½ t salt.

• Bring to a boil then reduce heat and simmer very gently, stirring occasionally, until most of the liquid is evaporated, the fat has been rendered and the meat is tender 1-1 ½ hours. If there is a lot of liquid, turn up the heat to boil it off, stirring to keep the pork from sticking.

• The meat can be cooked ahead to this point. If there is a lot of fat, drain it into a bowl, let it cool, discard the fat and add back any "juices". When the pork cools a bit, pull out any large pieces of gristle and fat and discard. Use a fork to pull apart the chunks.

• While the pork cooks, sliver the onion super thin and just 1" long. Sauté on medium about 8 minutes, stirring occasionally. Salt to taste and add ½ cup of the wine. Let it mostly boil off. Pour a little wine into a glass for the cook. Reserve 1-1 ½ more cups for the recipe and enjoy the rest.

• Let the onions cook slowly, covered for 15-20 minutes. Stir 3-4 times.

• Once the onions are very limp, combine them, ¾ cup fig balsamic vinegar, and a cup of the wine with the pork (or other meat). Cover, bring to a simmer and cook 1+ hours. Serve with warm 5" tortillas, tortilla chips, in wonton or lettuce cups, or your choice.

Red Wine Pasta with Broccoli

This is one of those dishes that is not only delicious, but also unusually beautiful. It is quick to prepare, as well (about 45 minutes), but does require attention and action most of the time, and two burners. As always, I prefer farmer-direct broccoli, and I like to use lots of it! Phillips Farms in Lodi, California has broccoli with small stems, and wonderful flavor and texture.

INGREDIENTS

Makes 6-8 main course servings

2-4 lbs broccoli, thick stems discarded

16 oz good quality pasta

1 750 ml bottle Zinfandel or Syrah

1+ t sugar, if wine is not fruity

3-5 T olive oil

6 cloves garlic, minced (2 T)

¾ t red pepper flakes

¾ t salt

½ t black pepper

1 - 2 oz (½-1 cup) finely grated parmesan

COOK'S NOTES

• If a vegetarian main course sounds intimidating, consider adding some seared shrimp or scallops blackened on the edges and then sliced into coins. However, with a hearty salad, such as Caesar, and a rich starter (warm cheese dip, chopped liver) you've got a wonderful meal. It can also make a very nice side dish.

PREPARATION

• Bring 3 quarts of water and 1-2 t salt to boil in a 6 quart pan.

• Cut broccoli into 1 inch florets and stems into ½" chunks.

• Blanch broccoli in the water for 2 minutes. If using 4 lbs, do it in two batches. It should still be crunchy. Transfer with a slotted spoon to a colander or rimmed baking tray to drain/cool.

• Reserve the cooking liquid, keep it at a boil, and add the pasta. It isn't much water, but this is correct. From the reboil, cook the pasta 4 minutes less than the package directions say, stirring occasionally.

• When draining pasta, save 1½ cups of the cooking water, as it will be needed later.

• In a large skillet, boil the wine and sugar vigorously for 4 minutes. Add the drained, par-cooked pasta and keep at a boil. Partially cover the pan.

• Shake the pasta wine pan repeatedly; stirring gently only if the shape requires it. Cook 4-10 minutes until barely al dente. If the pasta is running out of liquid, add some of the pasta cooking water. Keep it at a gentle boil and mostly covered.

• Meanwhile, in the now empty pasta pot, carefully cook the garlic, red pepper flakes, and olive oil over medium until the garlic is pale golden, 1- 2 minutes. Watch carefully, as it burns quickly.

• When the pasta is nearly cooked, increase the heat on the garlic and add the broccoli, salt, pepper, and more olive oil, and cook, tossing to bring the broccoli to a sizzle, 1-2 minutes.

• Combine the pasta and broccoli and let meld 1-2 minutes.

• Remove from heat and stir in cheese.

• Serve within 5 minutes.

Rabe, Sausage & White Bean Pasta

Rabe is very popular in Italian cuisine, but not very well known in this country. It resembles broccoli but has thinner stems, smaller heads, and a slightly stonger flavor that goes well with the sausage in this recipe. This quick and easy dish is a perfect full meal in itself, though it could be accompanied by a bold winter salad such as Caesar or radicchio and escarole with a mustardy vinaigrette.

INGREDIENTS

Serves 5-7

2-3 lbs broccoli rabe

1 lb spicy sausage - raw is best

6 cloves garlic

Sea salt & fresh ground pepper

½ t red pepper flakes, more to taste

2-3 t fennel seeds if not in sausage

1 cup dry white beans, soaked and cooked

OR 2 cans well rinsed beans

1-2 c broth (bean cooking liquid is great)

12 oz dry pasta

1 juicy lemon; Meyer is great if available

2-3 oz grated good parmesan or pecorino cheese

optional - toasted bread crumb croutons

COOK'S NOTES

• The beans or the sausage can be omitted. If you don't use sausage, add red pepper flakes and fennel to taste.

• A short chunky pasta is good as it will catch the bits well. Sprouted or whole wheat pasta are also nice as their earthy flavor and "coarser" texture work well with the other ingredients.

PREPARATION

• Boil 4 quarts salted water.

• Sauté sausage in a large pan.

• Chop garlic and add to sausage.

• Add salt, pepper, red pepper flakes, and fennel if needed.

• Clean rabe, separating stems. Discard any woody stems with a white core. Chops stems into ⅓" slices, chop the rest (flowers and leaves) into 1-2" pieces and keep separate.

• In the pasta water, boil stems 6 minutes plus half the leaves and flowers 3 minutes. The rest will go in at the end.

• Scoop rabe out with a metal sieve or slotted spoon. Add to sausage as well as ½ cup broth or pasta water.

• Add water to pasta pot if needed and reboil. Add pasta and, once it boils, set the timer according to the package directions.

• When the pasta goes in, add the beans and another ½ cup broth to the simmering sausage rabe mixture.

• Grate in the lemon peel and add the juice from ½ the lemon. Taste and season as needed. Some of the rabe should be almost disintegrating.

• When pasta looks 3 minutes from al dente, add the remaining rabe to the water. Cook it all two more minutes, drain, and save 1 cup water.

• Combine the sausage and pasta mixture.

• Simmer the mixture 2-4 minutes, stirring gently. The rabe should be turning to mush, even giving the pasta a greenish cast.

• Once it looks and tastes to your liking, turn off the heat and grate in half of the cheese. Serve the remaining cheese as a topping with the toasted bread crumbs.

Chili "Tamale" Pie

This recipe is a throwback from the late 1980's. It is so good after a cold day in the outdoors! I made it with a red corn polenta which has an unusual blue color when ground, and cooks to a deep lavendar or purple, but any good polenta will do. The corn bread topping is made without extra add-ins, so you can really experience the flavor and color of the corn. I recommend using heirloom "Rio Zape" or "Good Mother Stallard" beans, which also have interesting color and give the pie a rich, smoky flavor.

INGREDIENTS   *Fills a 9 x 13 inch baking dish*

THE CHILI

½ lb flavorful heirloom beans (recommend "Rio Zape" or "Good Mother Stallard")

1 T olive oil

1 large onion, chopped

2 large carrots, small chopped, optional

1-2 green/red sweet peppers, chopped

3 cloves garlic, minced

1 pound 95%-lean ground beef (or double the beans)

1 28-ounce can crushed tomatoes, undrained

3 T chili powder

1 T ground cumin

1 t smoked spanish paprika

¼ t cayenne pepper (optional)

THE CORNBREAD TOPPING

1 ¼ cups cornmeal

¾ c whole-wheat flour

1-2 T sugar

1 t baking powder

½ t baking soda

¼ t salt

1 large egg, lightly beaten

1 ¼ cups low-fat milk

2 T olive oil (more if desired)

½ cup chopped fresh cilantro, optional

1½ cups shredded extra-sharp cheddar, optional

COOK'S NOTES

- Beans can be cooked up to three days ahead.

- Chili can be prepared up to three days ahead. Bake the casserole for 50 minutes.

- The whole dish can be prepared ahead. If you do this, let it cool for 1 hour, then cover and refrigerate for up to 3 days. Before serving, remove it from the refrigerator and let it stand at room temperature for 45 minutes. Then reheat at 350 for 30-40 minutes.

continued on next page . . .

PREPARATION

THE CHILI

- Heat oil in a Dutch oven over medium heat. Add onion and cook until beginning to soften, about 4 minutes. Add carrot, bell pepper and garlic and cook 2 minutes. Add beef, breaking it up with a wooden spoon. Cook to brown some of it, 4 to 5 minutes. Stir in beans, tomatoes and their juice, chili powder, cumin, paprika and cayenne (if using).

- Bring to a boil; reduce heat to maintain a simmer, cover and cook until slightly thickened, about 20 minutes.

- Preheat oven to 350. Coat a 9-by-13-inch (or similar 3-qt) baking dish with cooking spray.

THE CORNBREAD

Do this as soon as you get a break on the chile so it can rest a bit.

- Whisk cornmeal, flour, sugar, baking powder, baking soda, and salt in a large bowl. Whisk egg, milk and oil in a medium bowl. Add the wet ingredients to the dry ingredients, along with cilantro, and stir until just combined. Let sit without stirring until ready to spread it on top of the chili.

- Transfer the chili to the prepared baking dish and sprinkle with cheese if using. Spread the cornbread batter evenly over the chili.

- Bake the casserole until the top springs back when touched lightly, 20 to 25 minutes. Let stand for 10 minutes before serving.

Marianne in San Miguel de Allende, Mexico, 2010

Polenta Spoon Pie

This is a takeoff on spoon bread, which is made with finer grained cornmeal and is a sort of polenta soufflé. Spoon Pie is more substantial, with an egg-enriched polenta crust plus a delicious filling. We love to eat this for breakfast before skiing or after a chilly sunrise session of windsurfing in the Delta. Filling ideas are endless - use what you have that is fresh and delicious! You want about 4 cups of cooked filling (3-4 lbs raw) per cup of raw polenta. I have provided three ideas below.

INGREDIENTS

Makes a 3 qt pan. Serves 8 as a main dish

FILLING IDEA 1

■ *Chix on Stix 2009*

12 oz onion

12 oz fennel

12 oz sausage

1 bunch chard (16 oz)

4 oz Beecher's fresh cheese
  curds (local cheese)

FILLING IDEA 2

■ *Tahoe March 2009*

12 oz morel mushrooms

12 oz red onion

16 oz asparagus

4 oz buffalo mozzarella

FILLING IDEA 3

■ *Delta Tamale Pie*

onions & chard

zucchini, roasted peppers

tomatoes, corn, black beans

1 T cumin, 1 t Mexican spices,
  1 T fresh oregano, 2 t coriander

4 oz sharp cheddar

PREPARATION

• Put water/broth, salt pepper, sugar into a deep saucepan. A three quart pan is good.

• While stirring, add polenta in a stream so it doesn't lump.

• Bring to a boil and turn down to the lowest heat so polenta steams and occasionally bubbles.

• Cook like this for 20 minutes (5-10 for finer grain), stirring every 2 minutes.

• After 20 minutes, add 1 cup milk or broth, and cook 5-10 more minutes.

• Add cheese and fresh herbs if using. Taste and season (salt, pepper, sugar) as desired.

• Polenta will continue to thicken and the top will dry out unless it is covered. Add more liquid if needed.

• Cool 10 minutes. Gently mix in beaten eggs.

• While the polenta is cooking, chop and sauté the filling ingredients, salting and peppering as needed.

• Preheat the oven to 350-375.

• Grease a 3 quart lasagna pan or multiple smaller round pie pans.

• Pour polenta into pan(s). Wait on toppings.

• Bake polenta; 25 minutes for small pans, 40 for big pans. Pie should lose most of its "jiggle" when done.

• Pull pie out of oven. Leaving a small edge, spoon filling on and push it into the polenta well.

• Sprinkle the cheese on top.

• Bake another 25-50 minutes until golden, bubbly and set. Let rest 15-30 minutes before serving.

Crab-Stuffed Shells with Peas, Leeks, and Lemon

These are luscious! The vegetables in the filling balance out the richness of the crab and cream sauce, and the lemon adds a fresh flavor and zing.

THE PASTA

• Bring a large pot of water to a boil. Add 1-2 t salt and pasta shells; cook 2 to 3 minutes less than package instructions. Drain, leaving a little water on the noodles. Put back in pan and shake to keep moist.

THE CREAM SAUCE

• Melt 4 T butter in a large saucepan over medium heat. When bubbling, add flour and turn to medium low. Cook, whisking almost constantly, 2-3 minutes.

• Whisk briskly and pour in 2 cups milk. Add the rest of the milk once it settles. Continue cooking with a watchful eye, stirring often until mixture bubbles and thickens, about 15 - 25 minutes. It is OK to turn heat to medium, but watch the sauce carefully.

• Remove from heat; stir in lemon juice, and season generously with salt and pepper.

THE FILLING AND TOPPING

• Clean and chop the leeks - white and pale-green parts only. Discard the tops or save for stock (wash well). Rinse the leeks well, running water into the top. Quarter lengthwise, cut into ¼-inch slices. Rinse and drain 2-3 times.

• Melt 1 T butter in a medium skillet over medium heat. Add leeks, and cook until soft, 6-8 minutes. Season with salt and pepper after 4 minutes. Turn off heat, add the peas and crab. Cover and refrigerate until ready to assemble.

• Chop parsley, peel and mince garlic. In a small bowl, stir together bread crumbs, seasonings and oil; set aside.

ASSEMBLY

• Preheat oven to 375 degrees if you plan to cook immediately.

• Stir 1 ½ cups cream sauce into reserved crab mixture. Pour another cup of sauce into the bottom of a greased 3 quart baking dish (or 2 smaller ones).

• Generously fill each pasta shell with crab mixture. Nestle in baking dish. Mix any remaining filling into sauce and spoon over shells.

• Cover and cook 25 minutes.

• Uncover, turn heat to broil, and sprinkle with breadcrumb mixture. Broil until the crumbs are golden, about 5 minutes.

• Let cool 15 minutes before serving.

INGREDIENTS

Serves 6-8
(about 40 stuffed shells)

8 oz jumbo pasta shells

sea salt and freshly ground pepper

5 T unsalted butter, used in 2 parts

4 T all-purpose flour

5½ c milk

juice of 1 ½ lemons - about ¼ cup

3-4 whole leeks (5 cups chopped)

1 c frozen peas - petite preferred

16 ounces lump crabmeat, picked over and rinsed

¾ c bread crumbs, preferably homemade

6 garlic cloves, minced

¼ c fresh flat-leaf parsley leaves

1 T extra-virgin olive oil

Soy Style Grilled Salmon

We love marinating salmon in this sauce. From about May to September, fresh wild salmon is available in our area. Our favorite is Sockeye, but we also enjoy King. We buy a 1½-2 lb piece and enjoy it for lunch the next day as well (plus often for one more snack). It can be broiled, baked, or grilled. It is especially delicious grilled on a cedar plank.

INGREDIENTS

1½ -2½ lbs wild salmon fillet
(5-8 oz per serving)

⅓ cup Indonesian Sweet Soy
per 2 lbs salmon

1 lemon, for nice look at
serving, optional

cedar grilling plank, optional

AT SERVING, OPTIONAL

3 scallions, chopped
(use white and green)

1 T toasted sesame seeds

MARINADE / SAUCE

Makes 2 cups

1 c soy sauce

½ c brown sugar

¼ c fresh lemon juice

2 T fresh ginger

1 T minced garlic

¼-1 t red pepper flakes

FOR A SAUCE AT SERVING

½ cup butter

OR 1-2 cups coconut milk

COOK'S NOTES

- There is no need to flip a fillet with this preparation, because the sauce forms an attractive glaze.

- Make the sauce ahead of time. It makes plenty, so there will be extra for several delicious "next times".

- Using the wood plank adds a slight smoked flavor and texture that is wonderful!

PREPARATION

- Rinse and pat dry the fish and set it skin side down in a Pyrex-type lasagna pan to marinade in.

- Shake the sauce to blend all the "bits" and then spoon on to the fish. Once the sauce rolls off, turn the fish over and gently rub the flesh into the sauce. Let fish rest 20-60 minutes.

- Refrigerate if the kitchen is warmer than 78 degrees.

- Grill the fish, as usual, if you have a method that works.

- If desired, sprinkle the cooked fish with green onions and toasted sesame seeds.

TO GRILL USING A CEDAR PLANK

- Soak the plank in water 30 minutes - 4 hours.

- Heat the grill leaving one section turned off.

- Put the plank over the heat with the cooking side down. After 5 minutes, turn the plank over and move it to the unheated section of the grill OR turn on the entire grill to low-medium heat.

- Drain the fish and put it on the plank. Decorate with lemon slices.

- Grill 10-18 minutes with the grill closed.

- Cooking time will depend on the grill. It will be longer if you're grilling other things at the same time.

- If desired, sprinkle the cooked fish with green onions and toasted sesame seeds before presenting.

continued on next page . . .

FOR A TRADITIONAL GRILL

• Grill the fish skin side down. There is no need to flip it.

• For best results, drain the fish and grill over indirect heat or on a medium-high heat (400) for 7-14 minutes.

• Check for doneness by gently probing with a fork and looking into the flakes.

• It is best to under-cook the fish, and let it rest, or put it back on heat (or microwave 30+ seconds) than overcook it.

• Have a clean parchment-lined tray or large platter ready to put the cooked fish on. When it is done, use a large metal spatula (or 2) to remove the fish from the skin. It may not come off all in one piece. Don't worry; this won't affect how it tastes.

MAKING THE MARINADE / SAUCE

• The marinade version of this sauce keeps in the refrigerator for months. Remember; never dip a dirty utensil into the sauce.

• This sauce, whether made as a marinade or a serving sauce is wonderful on mushrooms, fish, shellfish, beef, chicken, pork.

• For a marinade or soy-type sauce, combine all the ingredients and simmer 5 minutes.

• For a serving/finishing sauce, stir in cubed butter or coconut milk. Let it mellow a few minutes.

Fig Balsamic Glazed Salmon

Even cooked ahead of time and served at room temperature, this dish is still delicious. When broiling, your fish can go from undercooked to blackened in a minute, so plan to keep a close eye on it. I have included directions for roasting as well.

INGREDIENTS

Makes 4 6-oz servings

24 oz salmon fillets (adjust rub to actual amount you have)

2 large cloves garlic, minced

2 t rosemary, minced - fresh if possible

1 T olive oil - more if wild salmon

½ t salt

¼ t fresh ground black pepper

¼ cup thick Fig Balsamic Vinegar

PREPARATION

• Combine all ingredients except salmon.

• Cut fish into serving pieces. Rub ½ the sauce over all the flesh. Let rest 45 minutes in a cool place.

• Put in bottom of broiler tray. Put thinner pieces in the middle and thicker pieces on the edge. Broil on the highest level you can stand. Tail end pieces will take 4-5 minutes, thicker pieces, 6-9 minutes.

• Brush the other half of the marinade on after 4 minutes.

• Cook the minimum time and pull out. Check by sticking a knife into the center of both the thinnest and thickest pieces. If any pieces are raw, give them a few more minutes. It is better to under-cook and then put back in the oven for a few minutes, than to overcook fish.

• Fish should rest in a warm place 3-5 minutes before serving. It will continue to cook as it rests.

RECIPE MODIFICATION

• The salmon fillet can be left whole rather than cut before cooking.

• Lay the fillet on a parchment lined tray and bake it at 425 for 8-14 minutes depending on how thick it is. It may not get as crispy as the broiler method but you can turn the broiler on for the last 2 minutes. Just don't overcook it.

• Individual portions can also be baked. Allow 6-9 minutes and broil at the end if desired.

Lox and Leek Pasta

A stop at Newcastle Produce (just off I-80 east of Auburn, CA) turned up some lovely small leeks grown right there at Jan's farm. Then I was gifted some of friend Chef Buddy O'Dell's gravlax cured, cold-smoked salmon. Combined with local lemons and pasta, this made a fantastic ready-in-40-minutes dinner! A light, creamy, lemony experience.

INGREDIENTS

Makes 4-6 servings

8-10 oz spaghetti or thin fettuccine

8-10 oz lox (preferred) or smoked salmon

1-2 T butter

1½ lbs chopped leeks (start with 2-2½ lbs)

salt and pepper

½ cup white wine

juice of ½ lemon, more to taste as desired

1 cup frozen peas

16 oz well drained goat yogurt (about 8 oz) OR 5 oz fresh goat cheese

⅓ cup half & half OR ½ - ⅔ cup crème fraîche, plus pasta water as needed

1 T minced fresh dill (sub as desired)

PREPARATION

• Bring a 3 qt pot with water and 2+ t salt to boil.

• Sauté leeks in butter. Once they start to soften, salt and pepper to taste. Regulate heat so they cook, but don't brown much.

• Add wine and lemon juice. Boil down - may take 10 minutes. Turn pan to low once liquid is boiled off.

• Water should be boiling; add pasta. Stir gently a few times until water comes back to a boil. Regulate heat to keep a constant boil but not an explosion.

• Once pasta is in, add peas to the leek mixture to thaw. Turn heat up a little as needed.

• Chop salmon and dill.

• Once peas thaw, add goat cheese. Watch heat so cheese melts but doesn't boil.

• When pasta is done, drain it and save about ½ cup of the boiling water.

• Add the pasta to the leek/cheese pan and stir to coat. Taste and season as needed.

• Mix in ½ the salmon and ½ the dill and plate the meals.

• Sprinkle the rest of the salmon and the dill on top of each serving.

MODIFICATION IDEAS

• Try with shrimp, asparagus, zucchini, or red peppers.

INGREDIENTS

Makes a 3 quart Pyrex pan (about 8 hearty main servings)

DRESSING

2+ T olive oil

2-2½ cups small chopped onion, about 8 oz

12 oz cooked Italian or other savory sausage links, optional

½ cup minced celery (2-4 stalks)

3 T coarsely chopped garlic, about 8 cloves

2 lbs chopped tomatoes

salt and pepper

12 fresh sage leaves fine chopped (½ t dry)

1 T fresh fine chopped oregano (1 t dry)

⅓ cup dry white wine (optional)

2 lbs (about 8 cups) chopped or thin sliced zucchini

4 cups cooked cannellini or navy beans (two 15 oz cans, drained and rinsed OR 10 oz dry, cooked and seasoned)

PERSILLADE TOPPING

2 T olive oil

1 clove garlic, minced

1 cup fresh bread crumbs

salt and pepper

¼ cup minced fresh parsley/ mixed herbs

Zucchini Cassoulet

Traditional cassoulet is a hearty winter dish featuring duck, pork, lamb, as well as tomatoes, white beans and bread crumb crust. This is a wonderful and healthy adaptation of the French classic.

PREPARATION

• Chop onions and sausage into thumbnail sized pieces, celery into pinky-nail size, and coarse chop the garlic. Once the onions are chopped, heat the oil in a 10-12" sauté or 6 quart pot and begin sautéing them on medium-medium/high. Add the sausage and celery. After the onions start to soften (about 5 minutes), salt and pepper to taste, stir and add the garlic. Cook 3 minutes.

• Chop and add the tomatoes, oregano and sage. Cook 5-7 min. Salt and pepper to taste again. Add the wine and cook down another 5-8 minutes. Turn down if it gets dry-ish.

• While this is cooking, chop the zucchini and heat ¾" of water in a sauté pan that has a lid. Add ½ t salt to the water and bring to a boil. In two batches, par cook the zucchini, covered, 3-4 minutes each. Put in a colander once it is cooked.

• Turn oven on to 375.

• Once zucchini is done, prepare persillade topping in same pan (see below).

• Mash ½ of the beans and then add all the beans to the tomato mixture. Taste and adjust seasoning as needed. Cook 3-5 minutes. If the mixture is soupy, pour off and save any extra liquid.

• Grease a 3 quart Pyrex "lasagna" pan (or 2 smaller ones) and sprinkle in a thin layer of breadcrumbs. Layer beans - zucchini - beans. Put 70% of persillade on top.

• Bake 30 min. Push crumbs into beans. Pour any reserved liquid over top.

• Put rest of crumbs on and bake 15 minutes. Carefully broil if desired.

PERSILLADE PREP

• Tear up 3-4 slices of good bread (multi-grain is best) and toss into a blender. Pulse and stir to get it all chopped up.

• Mince the garlic and gently cook in olive oil. When it softens, turn heat up a bit and add breadcrumbs, salt and pepper. Cook 3-5 minutes, stirring often until crumbs are golden.

• Chop the herbs and add in last 30 seconds.

COOK'S NOTES

• Persillade and zucchini can be prepared ahead.

• If using dry beans, remember to cook ahead.

• Leave out the sausage, and this is a vegan's delight.

Paella

If you like seafood and really want to impress friends and family at your next big get together, this is the entrée to do it with. I combined many recipes to create this signature dish. It is not really complex, but has many steps, dirties a lot of pans, and takes a bit of time. The result is worth every bit of effort — the flavors are deep and bold, and the presentation makes an impact.

INGREDIENTS

Makes 20-26 large servings, or 50 sides

EQUIPMENT NEEDED

• slant sided saute pan

• domed lid

• 6 qt stock pot

• 3-4 c heavy saucepan for saffron toasting, wine

BROTH BASE

3½ quarts water

will need 9½ c broth for full recipe

1-3 T bouillion base as needed to flavor broth

4 crushed bay leaves

bones, shells, vegetable scraps as they appear

SAFFRON MIX

1½ cup white wine

1-2 t saffron (½-1 gram)

MEAT & VEGETABLES

2 red peppers OR one 8 oz jar roasted peeled red peppers

1½ lb pork or soy chorizo sausage

1½ lbs (Stockton red or) yellow onions 4 cloves garlic

0-½ c olive oil

sea salt and fresh ground black pepper

one 4+ lb whole chicken/rabbit or 2¼ lbs chopped

1½ lb wild shrimp, monkfish, or halibut (or both)

18 oz can cooked legumes (1½ cups) or fresh beans

6-8 really big unpeeled shrimp for the top

OPTIONAL SHELLFISH

1-2 lbs mussels for the top

1-2 lbs clams in shell for the top

12-30 more unpeeled shrimp for the top

VEGETARIAN OPTIONS

1½ lbs quartered mushrooms (to replace top shrimp)

12 oz artichoke hearts

12 oz green beans

12 oz more legumes or other vegetables sauteed and added to onion/chorizo mix

AT ASSEMBLY

8-12 T lemon juice, ½ at a time

10 T chopped parsley (1 med bunch) ½ at a time

1¼ lbs tomatoes (3 c chopped)

5 cups round short grain Valencian Paella rice

2½ t smoked paprika

FINAL REHEAT

½ - ⅔ cup (3 oz) green peas (thawed, if frozen)

AT SERVING

reserved lemon juice & parsley

1-2 baguettes - sliced thinly

lemon wedges for garnish, optional

PREPARATION

• Roast peppers 20 minutes in a 400 oven or over a grill. Cool in a paper bag (or wrapped in parchment) in a plastic bag. Cook beans if making from scratch.

• Fill stock pot with 3 qts water and broth base ingredients. Cover, bring to a boil, uncover and keep at a low boil. Be sure to have all the cooking equipment ready.

• Toast saffron gently in the small pan. When aroma is released, add wine, bring to a boil and remove from heat. This will go onto rice after it sautes in chorizo mix.

• Chop onions, garlic and red peppers. Add scraps to stock.

• Optional: Set aside 8-12 long slices pepper for the top decoration.

• Heat the paellera (paella cooking pan). Saute chorizo & onions over medium heat, breaking up into little pieces. No oil is needed for pork. Use 3-4 T oil for soy chorizo.

• Once things are soft and beginning to brown, add red pepper, garlic, salt & pepper.

continued next page . . .

- Chop parsley, peel, seed, grate or mince tomato, and juice lemons. Put each in their own bowl Add bits to gently boiling stock pot.

- As chorizo cooks, chop chicken. Skin and cut into pieces. Discard wing tips and skin. Cut meat from breasts, back into large bite chunks, and most from thigh. Separate 2 wing pieces, drumsticks and thighs. Trim thighs. For a large paella, you now have 8 "bone" pieces. Don't toss bone pieces, saute them too and them add to stock.

- Remove some chorizo to the colander that's been set over the large bowl, making room for the chicken. Sear chicken on medium. You want to color it, not cook it through. Salt & pepper as it cooks. Bite-size pieces take 4-5 min, bone pieces 8-15. Add drained grease as needed.

- If using artichoke hearts or mushrooms, quarter, saute and season, as with the chicken.

- Peel and chop the seafood. Leave BIG shrimp for the top unpeeled. Add to red pepper slices for top decoration. Add shells to the stock, mix chopped and smaller pieces into cooked chorizo.

- Remove chicken pieces from paellera as they are done. Add boneless bites to chorizo and reserve "bone" pieces with unpeeled shrimp and red pepper slices for decorating the top of the paella at serving.

- If using fish chunks, quick saute in chorizo grease to color, not cook through. Salt & pepper. Remove from pan, keep in a separate container.

- Drain & rinse cooked legumes/chop raw green beans. Stir into chorizo mixture.

- Strain broth into chorizo bowl. Check seasonings. Rinse stock pot and return broth to pot. Keep warm if cooking paella right away.

COOKING PAELLA

- Reheat broth and chop parsley, tomatoes (if not done). Put chorizo mix (including chopped shrimp) back in pan & turn on medium. Taste to make sure it is well seasoned. When it sizzles, add rice. Mix gently to coat with chorizo oil.

- Add paprika (1 scant T), chopped tomato, ½ the parsley.

- Add 5 T lemon juice and the saffron wine mix. Stir and wow at the color change.

- Add 1 ⅞ cups broth per cup of rice. Shake pan to settle rice. Drop in fish pieces if using. Bring it to a gentle boil. Get the flame low, just enough to boil the edges.

- Turn heat to a simmer. Cover & cook 12 minutes. DO NOT STIR! Rice should be bubbling, not burning.

- If using, push bone meats and red pepper strips, into an attractive design.

- Rotate pan 180 degrees. Remember bone meats are not cooked through yet.

- Cook covered 10 more minutes. DO NOT STIR!

- Rotate pan again. Arrange big shrimp into the design. Sprinkle on peas, mussels, and clams if using.

- Cook covered or uncovered 6-15 more minutes until done.

- Remove lid once mussels & clams are cooked to let some of the water they make steam off.

- To test for doneness, use a fork & taste rice from the edges; the center cooks faster. If it seems uncooked, and the center is done but not soupy, add 1-2 T broth to the edges .Give it 7-8 more minutes. Don't over moisten. Patience and a low, even flame are key.

- Once the paella appears done, let it rest 5 minutes with burner off and lid on. If it is soupy, take the lid off, or put it in a 325 oven to "dry out"- DO NOT STIR!

- Paella can rest, not cook, in a warm spot up to an hour. Remove lid for part of the time.

- If needed, gently reheat covered 7-15 minutes just before serving. DO NOT STIR!

- If you wish, broil the top like they do in Sevilla.

- At serving, sprinkle rest of lemon juice and parsley over paella.

- Best to use a serving fork and flat round serving spoon to serve.

- *ENJOY!*

Strata

I am always looking for "make ahead and enjoy for a few mornings" breakfast recipes. This egg, bread, cheese, plus 'you choose' recipe has, therefore, migrated to my breakfast file. Whatever meal you serve it for, use great ingredients and everyone will love it!

PREPARATION

- Preheat oven to 250.
- Chop bread to 1 inch pieces. Put on parchment-lined cookie tray. Bake 30-40 minutes to dry out. Let the bread cool on the tray to continue drying out.
- Chop and sauté filling as needed. Season with sea salt and fresh ground pepper as you cook it. Add fresh or dry herbs to taste.
- Grate cheese(s).
- Beat eggs and milk, salt and hot pepper sauce.
- Grease baking dish with butter or olive oil.

TWO OPTIONS FOR ASSEMBLING THE DISH

❶
- Make a layer of most of the bread, then most of the filling, and then about ½ the cheese. Next layer the rest of the bread, filling and cheese. Pour the egg mixture over top.
- Press the bread down so it is covered by and soaks up the egg.

❷
- Mix all the bread, ½ the filling and ½ the cheese into the egg mixture. Pour half into the pan. Spread the other half of the filling and ½ the remaining cheese. Top with the rest of the egg mixture (custard), and finally, the rest of the cheese.
- The assembled dish should rest 30+ minutes before baking. It can be refrigerated up to 24 hours.
- Bake covered at 350 for 35 minutes, then 10-25+ more uncovered until golden, puffed, and solid. Check the center with a skewer. If your oven is full or the pan is really large, it could take up to 1 ½ hours.
- If using, sprinkle with fresh chopped herbs at serving.

INGREDIENTS

Fills a 13 x 9 pan (3 qt) or 2 large pie pans

Serves 8-10 as a main, 10-16 as side, 16 as lunch

16 oz of good, but somewhat stale bread

8-12 oz grated cheese (ideas below)

6-8 cups, 2½ lbs cooked filling (3½+ lbs raw). See next page for filling ideas.

6 eggs

3½ cups milk (2% or whole are best)

½ t sea salt and 6 splashes hot pepper sauce

fresh herbs to garnish

COOK'S NOTES

- Filling options are endless. I have noted several here, but I rarely make one that is exactly the same. Consider this recipe a template and take off from here.

- Prepared strata is best if it can rest 1 hour or overnight before baking. Plan to start it a day ahead, if you can. The flavors only get better every day, so it is a great make-ahead dish.

- This can be made in any size pan, just adjust cooking time.

- Save bits of good bread in the freezer. When you have enough, start planning a filling and who will be lucky enough to share it with you!

continued on next page . . .

Strata Filling Ideas

"TURKISH"

Use olive and regular bread

1 lb Diestel turkey sausage

1 giant fennel bulb, sliced

1 giant onion, med chop

8 oz chard leaves

1-2 red pepper match sticked (or 3 anaheims)

4-6 oz grated Pecorino Romano

6-8 oz feta, crumbled

2 c tomato sauce

- Sauté meat. Add fennel, onion, and finally chard.
- Sauté peppers separately.
- Layer bread, meat mixture, Pecorino, bread, peppers, egg mixture (push it all down to soak in), tomato sauce in dollops, and feta cheese.

HAM AND APPLE

2-2½ lbs apples peeled & sliced (makes 1¼-1½ lbs)

2 T sugar

½ t ground cinnamon to cover apple slices

12 oz ham

1 t thyme

1 t sage

6 oz jack or cheddar or combo

1½ t ground mustard powder

1 t Worcestershire sauce

- Thin slice apples. Toss with sugar and cinnamon.
- Sauté onion in butter - salt and pepper.
- Sauté ham (optional).
- Add herbs at end.
- Combine onions, apples, ham.
- Add mustard and Worcestershire to custard.

CRAB MUSHROOM

1½ lbs cleaned, thinly sliced mushrooms

2 t minced garlic

2 T olive oil

4 t sherry vinegar

3 T sherry

2 t fresh thyme

salt and pepper

⅔ c green onions

OR use leek and sauté with mushrooms

12-16 oz crab

6-8 oz Jack, Swiss, or Parrano cheese

- Sauté mushrooms and garlic in oil for 5 minutes. Add sherry, thyme, salt and pepper. Cook 5 more minutes.
- Chop green onion.
- Layer as in the second option.

CARAMELIZED ONION

3½ lbs onions

½ lb cheese - raclette or other gooey one

Dash nutmeg in custard

- Caramelize the onion in butter or oil
- Layer bread, then onions, then cheese. Pour custard on top.

PIZZA

8 oz chopped ham or salami

8 oz chopped mushrooms/peppers/olives

1 onion, about 6-8 oz

3 cloves garlic

2 t Italian seasoning,

14 oz can diced tomatoes

6 oz chard or spinach

- Use mozzarella & parmesan cheeses. Sprinkle with 2 T ea chopped parsley and capers to serve. Use some olive bread on this one!

MUSHROOM

1¾ lb fresh porcini

may substitute cultivated and 2 oz re-hydrated dry porcini

1½ lb Stockton or other red onion

1 lb Swiss chard

1 t sea salt, ½ t fresh ground pepper or to taste

2 t sherry vinegar, once sauté is dry

8 oz fresh buffalo mozzarella or jarlsberg

continued on next page . . .

🥘 PLATINUM "KITCHEN SINK"

1 lb fresh morel mushrooms

1 lb chard

5 oz bacon

sun-dried tomato

🥘 BROCCOLI AND SUN-DRIED TOMATO

3 onion bagels for the bread

16+ oz broccoli

7 oz bacon

7 oz baby Stockton red onions

20 halves dried tomatoes, re-hydrated

5 oz Pedrozo cheese (wow!!)

4 oz mozzarella

🥘 SKIER'S WEDDING BREAKFAST

Use olive and regular bread

4 lb Diestel turkey sausage

2 small fennel bulb, sliced

4 lbs mushrooms, chopped

4 giant onion med chop

14 oz chard kale mix

½ cup sun dried tomatoes, re-hydrated overnight

made 10 lbs cooked

12 oz sharp cheddar

• Sauté veggies and meat and season well.

• Layer as in the second option.

🥘 SUMMER GARDEN 9/10

12 oz onion sautéed

salt and pepper

1 lb cherry tomatoes

onions cooked 4 min & mashed

2 lb 12 oz zucchini steamed 2-3 minutes

6 oz pepper chopped 1 x ¼" tossed with hot zucchini

½ c fresh finely chopped basil

8 oz pecorino & smoked mozzarella

• Used just 3 cups milk

• Filled 3 quart + pie plate.

Fig Quesadillas

*T*hese delicious quesadillas are a favorite quick snack among friends and family. Served with rice and beans, or a salad, they can make a complete vegetarian meal.

INGREDIENTS

Makes 6 servings

6 flour tortillas

approximately 3 cups fresh figs, sliced ⅛ inch thick

1 large bunch of cilantro, stems removed, chopped fine

1 large red onion, minced

5 oz Jack cheese, grated

DIPPING SAUCE

½ c crema or crème fraîche or sour cream

1 - 2 limes

PREPARATION

• Preheat oven to 350.

• Place 3 tortillas on an un-greased cookie sheet.

• Place sliced figs on tortilla, as close together as possible so that entire surface of tortilla is covered.

• Sprinkle liberally with minced onion, chopped cilantro and grated cheese. Salt lightly.

• Place remaining three tortillas on top of each stack and press down slightly. Tuck back in any ingredients that fall out.

• Bake in oven until cheese is melted and onion becomes "jam-like".

• Let cool 5 minutes, before slicing in wedges.

• Combine crema or creme fraich with juice of one or two limes, to taste, and serve as a dipping sauce with quesadillas.

Sauces

Pestos – Traditional Genovese and Thai Basil Mint

If you have an abundance of basil in your garden or it is well priced at your local farmers' market, you have to make pesto! I like to make a double or triple batch and then freeze most of it for use over the winter. We slather what I don't freeze on just about everything for a couple of weeks. It is delicious, healthy, and fun to get creative with. There are as many pesto recipes as there are cooks. Here are two variations to try.

Traditional Pesto Genovese

INGREDIENTS

Makes about 1 cup

¼ cup pine nuts (pignoli), lightly toasted

½ cup freshly grated parmesan (about 2 oz)

2 cups tightly packed basil leaves with small stems (1-2 huge bunches)

3 cloves garlic or ½ head green garlic, coarse chop

¼ -⅓ t salt

¼ cup extra virgin olive oil or use ½ cup if you want a thinner pesto

¼ t fresh ground black pepper

PREPARATION

• Toast nuts over medium heat 3-4 minutes until they start to brown. Stir often to prevent burning

• Pick basil leaves from stems, and discard stems. Don't chop the leaves yet, so they won't turn black.

• Coarse chop garlic.

• Grate cheese finely in food processor. Switch to other blade and add cooling pine nuts, garlic and salt to the cheese. Process until smooth.

• Add basil leaves. Blend until processor won't chop any more.

• Drizzle in olive oil and continue to blend, Pulse in black pepper.

• Store in a narrow jar and cover the surface of the pesto with olive oil. Any parts exposed to air will turn black.

MODIFICATIONS

• Substitute tomato for some to most of the oil, cheese or pine nuts to lower fat content. It will be runnier.

SERVING IDEAS

• It's great drizzled over a platter of big sliced fresh garden tomatoes.

• Mix with chevre, shredded mozzarella and stuff cherry tomatoes with mixture.

• Stuff into mushrooms & broil.

• Layer crostini, pesto, tomato slice, mozzarella.

• Mix with butter, spread on bread, and broil.

• Thin with fresh pureed tomatoes or more oil and spoon on tomato slices or other salad items.

• Use a spoonful or so per serving to fortify a minestrone -type soup.

• Rub pesto onto slabs of zucchini or eggplant - or on a salmon fillet before grilling.

• Mix into ground beef for extra snazzy burgers.

• Feature in a pasta salad or hot pasta dish. A great winter dish is ravioli with cooked cauliflower and pesto.

• Add to sandwiches.

Thai Basil Mint Pesto

INGREDIENTS

Makes about 1 ½ cup

½ cup unsalted dry-roasted peanuts

1 serrano or 2 jalapeño chiles, seeded & chopped

1½ t finely chopped fresh ginger

1 t finely chopped garlic

2½-5 T fresh lime juice (I use 2½ T)

1½ T Asian fish sauce

1½ t sugar

½ t kosher salt (less if using salted peanuts)

6 T peanut or canola oil (or may use 4 T canola and 2 T sesame oil)

2 cups packed Thai (or regular) basil leaves

1 cup packed fresh mint leaves

PREPARATION

• Process peanuts in a food processor until very finely chopped, but not to peanut butter.

• Add next 7 ingredients (chile through salt). Process until smooth.

• With processor running, add oil in a slow stream. Process until the oil is incorporated.

• Add basil and mint. Pulse, scraping bowl as needed, to incorporate herbs.

• Taste and adjust seasoning and acidity. If needed, thin with a little water.

• This recipe doesn't discolor like traditional pesto.

• This makes an AMAZING rub on grilled salmon!

COOK'S NOTES

• These pestos come out with the consistency of thick peanut butter. They can be thinned by using more oil.

• The Genovese style can also be thinned by blending in a peeled seeded tomato or two.

• Either pesto is great as a wet rub on fish, and would probably be just as good on chicken, pork or steak.

• They work fantastically as a mix-in for hot pasta or a cold pasta salad.

• Pestos freeze well and are wonderful to pull out in the dead of winter. Either freeze in ice cube trays and transfer to a resealable bag, or fill 8 oz deli containers and cut out (carefully) as much as you need.

• Pesto turns black from oxidation with exposure to air. Don't spread it until the last minute.

Columbia River Steelhead fresh from Native American fisherman, 2007

Aioli

Here are three variations of the smooth creamy sauce known as aioli. The main difference here is that the aioli is loaded with garlic, while the herb mayonnaise is spiced with herbs, and the vegan version uses less oil.

Traditional aioli originated in southern France and is widely used in Mediterranean cuisine. You can dip veggies or fried food into it, spread it on sandwiches, fish, or use as a marinade for meat. It is heavenly stuff. Indulge!

BASIC INGREDIENTS

Makes 1 1/4 cups

1/2 cup best olive oil

1/2 cup canola oil

1 egg - room temp

1/16 t sugar - no more!

1/8 t white pepper

1/4 t dry mustard

¼- ½ t salt

1 t lemon juice

1 t white wine

FOR AIOLI
4 cloves FINE CHOPPED garlic or 3/4 head green garlic

FOR HERB MAYONNAISE
Add 2-6 T of one or a combination of well chopped herbs.

VEGAN VERSION
2 part SILKEN tofu to 1 part olive oil - may need more seasoning.

PREPARATION
• Combine everything in a deep, straight-sided container. Be sure garlic is well chopped!

• Blend without moving the device until the oil stops being drawn to the bottom.

• Angle the blender and slowly draw it upward through the mixture to fully emulsify.

• Will keep 3 weeks in fridge.

COOK'S NOTES

• An immersion blender, (Bamix, with blade B), is best for this recipe.

• Up to 6x the recipe quantity can be made at one time.

• Experiment with different oils or try adding some basil or olives to the mix.

Thai Apricot Basil Sauce

I first developed this sauce for serving with grilled wild shrimp at Michael-David Winery in Lodi (7 Deadly Zins++) for Zinfest weekend. It is also a great sauce for salmon, pork, lamb, or scallops. If you are grilling, don't put too much on, as the honey may cause flare ups. It is also excellent on toasted baguette slices atop a bit of chevre or cream cheese.

INGREDIENTS

1 lb chopped ripe apricots - about 3½ cups

2 t Thai red curry paste

2 T honey or agave nectar

1 oz basil leaves, no stems - about 1 gently packed cup

PREPARATION

• Combine everything in a food processor or use a hand- turned "salsa maker". Don't liquefy the apricots. Leave some chunks.

• The sauce is better after a few hours, even the next day.

• The basil does turn black after 2 or 3 days, but the flavor is still outstanding!

FOR ROASTED SALMON (OR OTHER FISH)

• Line a rimmed cookie tray with parchment and put the fillet(s) skin side down. Coat with the sauce - not so much that it slides off. Don't dip the utensil back in the sauce after it has touched the raw salmon. Let sit 5-20 minutes.

• Bake at 360 for about 20 minutes for a 1½ pound fillet. Use a fork to look at the flesh in the thickest part to make sure it is not still raw.

• Broil 2-3 minutes if desired.

FOR GRILLED MEATS / FISH

• Very lightly brush some of the sauce on the meat up to an hour ahead of time. Grill the meat and serve with the sauce as a relish.

FOR SHELLFISH

• Toss the shrimp or scallops in the sauce and let sit 5-30 minutes. Pan fry or roast as with the salmon, on parchment-lined trays. This will only take 10-15 minutes.

• You can roast it at a higher temperature if desired, and finish under the broiler for color and crisping.

Cilantro Chutney

I bought a big bunch of cilantro at the farmers' market last week for another recipe and needed to use the remainder. And, with the mint growing in my garden, this recipe made great use of what I had.

Dave grilled zucchini that I'd rubbed with olive oil, salt and pepper. Then I spread this sauce on and let it sit for about 10 minutes before we ate. Tonight we'll do the same with lamb chops. I also want to try it on a potato salad and on tomatoes — mmmm!

INGREDIENTS

Makes about ⅔ cup

2 c well packed cilantro sprigs

1 c packed mint leaves

2 scallions, chopped coarsely

1 stemmed serrano,
  more to taste

OR

3 stemmed jalapeños,
  more to taste

0-3 t sugar

½ t salt

1-2 T lemon/lime juice

1 T veg oil

PREPARATION

• Process all except liquids to a thick paste.

• Add lime and oil and blend to smooth.

• Taste and adjust seasonings.

COOK'S NOTES

• This makes a lovely smooth electric green sauce, but using the term chutney clues us into the fact that there will be a sweet/sour taste to the sauce.

• It's wonderful on grilled meats and vegetables and would be an amazing base for a lettuce or vegetable salad dressing.

Delectable
Desserts

Clafoutis - French Fruit-Filled Cake

This is a summer favorite. Standard recipes for Clafoutis use a lot less fruit, but my nectarine tree is so productive and we think that more fruit and less cake is healthier, not to mention more delicious. I usually make three cakes at a time, so we can share one with a helpful friend or neighbor, and still have plenty for us. And, like crisp and pie, it is excellent for breakfast as well as dessert. Yum!

INGREDIENTS

Makes a 9" round pie or 6-8 servings

THE BATTER

6 T butter, melted

2 eggs, can use 3 for a
    double batch

1 t vanilla

⅓ cup milk

½ cup sugar

1 cup flour, can use ½ whole
    wheat

1 t baking powder

¼ t salt

1 T sugar, just after baking,
    optional

THE FRUIT

1½-2 lbs fruit (need 16-22 oz
    chopped). Only make this
    with delicious ripe fruit.

• Cherry - this is the classic, but
    I usually make clafoutis swith
    stone fruit. For extra heaven,
    roll each piece of fruit in sugar
    before putting into the batter.

• Nectarine, peach, blueberry,
    plum, figs, apples - all
    work well. Try different
    combinations.

PREPARATION

MAKE BATTER - BEST IF DONE THE NIGHT BEFORE

• Grease a 9" pie pan or other cooking pan.

• Melt butter.

• Whisk eggs, vanilla and milk. Add butter.

• Stir dry ingredients in smaller bowl. Add dry to wet and stir with
    large fork to just mix.

• Let rest 30 minutes - 36 hours in fridge, preferably overnight in the
    pre-greased pie pan.

• If you can't rest the batter in the baking pan, it's okay. Just stir
    minimally when you transfer it.

PREP FRUIT, ASSEMBLE AND BAKE

• Preheat oven to 375. Set a piece of parchment or old tray on the
    oven rack to catch any drips.

• Slice each fruit into 6-10 wedges depending on its size.

• Remove batter from refrigerator.

• Set fruit slices in batter standing them up, very close together, so
    they will stand up. Start with 4-6 pieces right in the middle. Hold
    them up as best you can while putting a ring around the outside
    edge. Then put a ring around the center group keeping them
    all standing up as best you can. Then place additional rings of
    fruit around one another. This method keeps the batter evenly
    dispersed. It takes some practice, but don't stress it. You could just
    lay the segments down, but I like to fit in more fruit and the cake
    will puff up around the standing pieces. If you're using more than
    one kind of fruit, create a pattern—make it beautiful.

• Bake 35-45 minutes on the parchment or tray (longer for multiple
    cakes). Rotate 180ª after 20 minutes. If after 45 minutes it seems
    95% done, turn off the oven and leave the cake in for 5-8 minutes.
    Or keep baking it. If it seems really golden but is not set after 35
    minutes, turn oven down to 350 and give it another 15-25 minutes.

• Optional: sprinkle hot clafoutis with 1 T sugar.

Fruit Sorbet

Overripe and imperfect fruit is great for making sorbets. Freeze the super ripe pieces until you are ready to use them. Sorbets typically have some kind of liqueur with the fruit. Since we have a nectarine tree and get great strawberries at Hmong Farmstands, we like to use that fruit combination with Triple Sec. Persimmon sorbet with dark rum is amazing, too. (See the recipe on the next page).

These desserts aren't difficult to make. They leave a wonderful taste on the tongue and really do cool you down on a hot day.

This recipe is just a starting point. Let your imagination run wild with flavor combinations.

INGREDIENTS

Makes 2-2 ½ cups

1 ¼ lbs fruit
(to make 1 lb chopped)

½ cup water

¼ cup sugar

3 T liqueur

3+ T half & half, yogurt, cream cheese, or crème fraiche, optional

PREPARATION

- Peel fruit and chop into cherry sized pieces. Spread in a single layer on a parchment-lined tray. Be sure it will fit in the freezer.
- Freeze 4+ hours. Once the pieces are frozen, transfer them to a bag and leave in the freezer.
- Combine the water and sugar in a small saucepan and simmer one minute, stirring gently to dissolve the sugar. Let this simple syrup cool 30+ minutes.
- While the syrup cools, remove fruit from freezer and let sit at room temperature 5 minutes.
- In a food processor, combine the fruit, simple syrup and liqueur. Mix well, stopping to stir down the bowl as needed. Add dairy, if using.
- The longer you blend the mixture, the creamier it gets. Scrape mixture into a shallow container and freeze 2+ hours. Plan to let the sorbet sit at room temperature a few minutes before serving. This time can vary, as you will see.

INGREDIENT NOTES

- Adding dairy technically makes this a sherbet or gelato. I think adding just this small amount makes the sorbet smoother. If you want an icier product, don't add the dairy.
- The liqueur makes the sorbet not freeze as hard. Leave it out if desired, but it does add some interesting flavors, and I like including it. Adjust sweetness to taste.

FLAVOR IDEAS

- Nectarines & Strawberries with Triple Sec or Grand Marnier
- Cherries with Crème de Cassis
- Peaches and Strawberries with Amaretto
- Strawberries and Bananas with Port
- Nectarines & Raspberries (3 oz) with Crème de Cassis and Orange liqueur - no dairy

COOK'S NOTES

- This requires really ripe, sweet fruit.
- Too much sugar makes it loose, too little sugar makes it icy.
- Lemon juice brings out the flavors.
- Keep sugar syrup strong - try 1 c water to ¾ c sugar.
- The sugar syrup can be made ahead of time.
- The processed sorbet needs to freeze 2+ hours to harden, but do enjoy a few spoonfuls or even a bowl right away. It will just be a little soft.
- A food processor is needed.

Peach Gelato

Gelato is an Italian ice cream made with dairy, sugar, and other flavorings such as fruit or chocolate.

INGREDIENTS
Makes 4-6 cups

1.5 pounds peeled, pitted peaches OR use nectarines, cherries or other fruits

½ pint strawberries (optional)

¼ + cup sugar, to taste

½ cup mascarpone, crème fraiche, yogurt, or heavy cream

PREPARATION

• Cut peaches/berries into very small pieces. The smaller, the smoother the gelato.

• Spread in a single layer on a rimmed cookie tray lined with parchment. Make sure the tray will fit in the freezer. Freeze solid, 2+ hours.

• Grind frozen fruit and sugar in food processor. Add dairy and pulse until mixture is as smooth as desired.

• Empty gelato into small container and refreeze.

• Serve as is or reprocess, if desired.

Persimmon Sherbet

By definition, sherbet is a frozen dessert with 1-2% milk product. It can work with or without the added dairy, but for this "decadent" recipe, keep it in.

INGREDIENTS
Makes 4-6 cups

24 oz peeled persimmons - 2+ lbs whole

6-8 T sugar

½ cup water

½ t vanilla extract

3 T dark rum

½- cup half & half (or crème fraiche)

PREPARATION

• Line a flat tray with parchment paper. Make sure it can fit in the freezer.

• Peel, chop & freeze persimmons. Once they are solid, break them into pieces and transfer to a freezer storage bag until ready to use. If the whole unpeeled fruit frozen, that's OK. You just need to pull them out and let them partially thaw. As soon as you can handle them, peel, chop and refreeze them, not to rock hard, but close.

• Bring water and 6 T sugar to a simmer and cook until all sugar melts. Don't stir or sugar will burn on sides of the pan. Let cool to room temperature.

• Remove frozen chopped fruit from freezer and let thaw for about 10 minutes.

• Process ingredients in order - fruit and sugar water for a while, then rum and extract. Taste and add extra 2 T sugar, if needed. Add the cream last, once the mixture is already smooth.

• Freeze 2+ hours.

Index

Made in the USA
San Bernardino, CA
24 May 2016